◆ LARRY A. HEIDELBERG ◆

REVELATION
Questions Answered
"Promised before the world began"

ISBN: 978-1-963851-95-3 (Paperback)
978-1-963851-96-0 (Hardback)
978-1-963851-97-7 (Ebook)

Olympus Story House

Contents

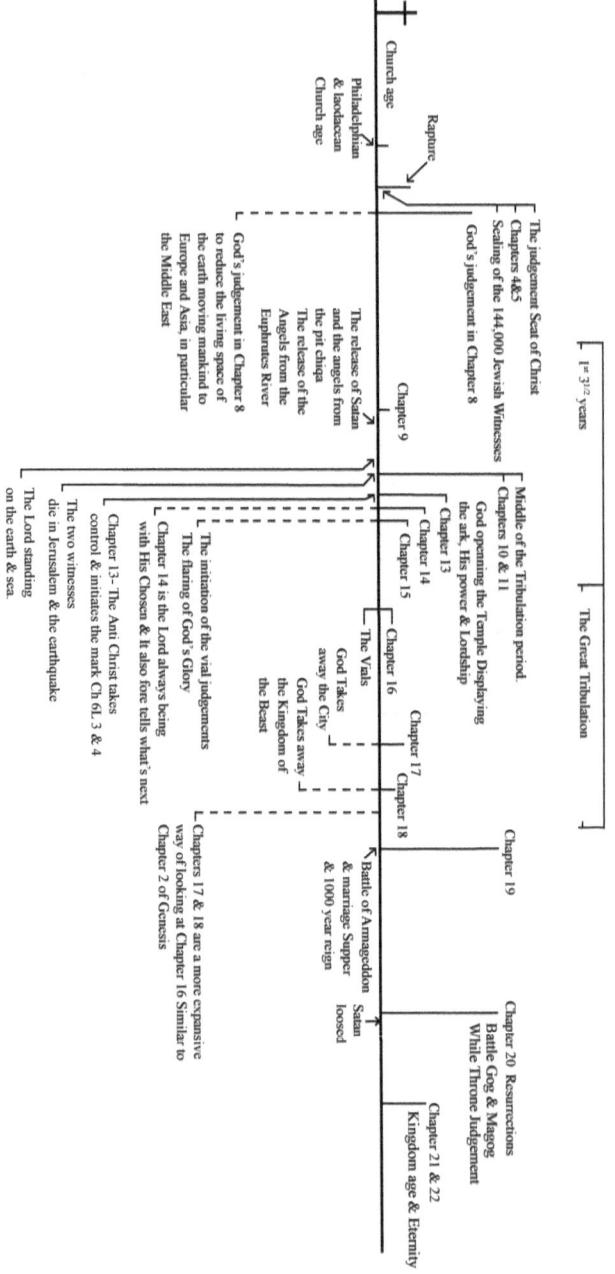

Chapter 1

There have been many books written on the Book of Revelation of the Holy Bible.

I have read some and heard many messages using this book as text. I have taught the Book of Revelation in church services and preached from it myself But I did nor want this book to be a combination of other people's works. I had so many questions about the different events and sequences covered in this fascinating and encouraging book of God. The other writers did nor answer those questions. I did not have these answers until a few months ago. I started writing this work in early 2003, did a bunch of editing in 2007 and 2008, and am now finishing it in 2020.

While I was in Baptist Bible College, Dr. Noel Smith encouraged me and all the students to think for ourselves. Well, I had already been guilty of that, but he sure caused it to sink home.

I have only studied the Word of God in preparation for this book. Do I remember some things of others' writings? Yes, but I am not going to use them here, as you will see in what is revealed. I think you will enjoy my book because of the answers to my, and possibly to your, questions.

To the child of God, the Book of Revelation should be of great encouragement, because God is in control. It shows us how He will bring an end to evil, and we can see the glorious life we will have with Him. To the person who has nor accepted the Lord Jesus Christ as their Savior, the Book of Revelation should scare you "serious." the events of this book could start unfolding any second. I cover Revelation on a commentary- and expository-type study basis. If that is not proper, I am sorry; it just came out that way.

> 1. *The Revelation of Jesus Christ, which God gave unto him, to shew unto his servants things which must shortly come to pass; and he sent and signified it by his angel unto his servant John:*
> 2. *Who bare record of the word of God, and of the testimony of Jesus Christ, and of all things that he saw.*
> 3. *Blessed is he that readeth, and they; that hear the words of this prophecy, and keep those things which are written therein: for the time is at hand.*

What first comes to my mind, besides the obvious necessity of studying the Book of Revelation, is something I handled more thoroughly in my book on the Book of Hebrews. That is the humility of Jesus. It must not be confused with His humanity, even though they are so closely related. To use Micah 5:2: *"But thou, Bethlehem Ephratah, though thou be little among the thousands of Judah, yet out of thee shall he come forth unto me that is to be ruler in Israel; whose going forth have been from of old, from everlasting."*

When John writes, "which God gave unto him," in 1:1, what is seen is the humility of the man Jesus. There was not first God and later the being Jesus coming along; neither was there the Father and then Jesus. But we dealt with that enough in that former book. Let me say that the human being Jesus, God the Son (God in the flesh), had a job to do, and that was to present a holy kingdom to satisfy the demands of the Godhead. John 5:22f, 27 says, *"For the Father judgeth no man, but hath committed all judgment unto the Son: That all men should honor the Son, even as they honor the Father. He that honoureth not the Son honoureth not the Father which hath sent the Son Anhdath given him authority to execute judgment also, because he is the Son of man."*

Author's note when an J' is used after a verse number it means the verse following also. When an 'f' is used after a verse number it means to continue to the end of the chapter.

God the Father is used as the focal point in Jesus' words and life while here on earth. In the Book of Revelation, God the Father is not mentioned by name. What is seen is Christ's job of presenting a glorious kingdom to the Godhead.

As from the moment of creation, and as seen in Revelation, God the Holy Spirit is the hands-on Godhead member in our lives. We must keep in mind that each member of the Godhead is frilly equal to the other two. They have their individual jobs to do in accomplishing their goal of sharing the Life and Love of the Godhead with those who will accept the Godhead on the Godhead's terms.

We will later see what happens to those who will not accept the Godhead on their terms. In this chapter, we see the magnificence of the humbled One, His glory and His majesty. In the Book of Revelation, the Lord Jesus Christ is seen on many occasions in His different functions, all at the same time.

The apostle John is writing what he is being shown and told to write. Let me point out the empowering of John by using the following passage. Second Peter 1:21 reads, *"For the prophecy came not in old time by the will of man: but holy men of God spake as they were moved by the Holy Ghost."* Might I point out here that the very God who created would certainly be able to bring about His love letter to His creation. Because He is Jehovah, He would have to do just that.

Let's get started with verses 4–8:

> 4. *John to the seven churches which are in Asia: Grace be unto you, and peace, from him which is, and which was, and which is to come; and from the seven Spirits which are before his throne;*
> 5. *And from Jesus Christ, who is the faithful witness, and the first begotten of the dead, and the prince of the kings of the earth. Unto him that loved us, and washed us from our sins in his own blood,*
> 6. *And hath made us kings and priests unto God and his Father; to him be glory and dominion for ever and ever. Amen.*

7. Behold, he cometh with clouds; and every eye shall see him, and they also which pierced him: and all kindreds of the earth shall wail because of him. Even so, Amen.

8. I am Alpha and Omega, the beginning and the ending, saith the Lord, which is, and which was, and which is to come, the Almighty.

Verses 4—5 show two views of the Lord Jesus Christ. Remembering verse 1, we must realize that Jesus Christ is the focal point of Revelation. We must keep in mind that one of the purposes of the Bible is to bring about a righteous kingdom. In verse 4, we see the ressurected One. We see that the One who was must be the One who died; this scripture shows this and it will be seen again later. In verse 5, that same person is shown not only as Jesus the life-giver, but also as Christ the payment for sin. What is brought forth in these two verses is ownership. Jesus Christ has the authority, but even more to the point, He met the price of the cost of creation's peace *"and washed us from our sins in his own blood"* (v. 5). The grandeur of the One who opens this scene befits the One who has all power. He met our need of being bought back from sin; hence, He is the judge of the use of that payment.

The Lord is causing to be written in total frankness about His authority, His message, and to whom and of the effect it will have across the globe. The divinity of the Lord Jesus and the magnitude of the importance of the coming message should easily befelt. Matthew 28:18 comes full-faced to us with an even greater impact: *"And Jesus came and spake unto them, saying, All power is given unto me in heaven and in earth."*

In these verses, we see the Lord Jesus Christ in glory and ownership, not because of ego, but in the design of the Godhead and for the glory of the Godhead. He is pictured as the judge. These verses, this chapter, and this book bringout the credentials of the Lord as judge. We see God the Son as the message-giver, God the Holy Spirit as the omnipresent One, and God the Father as the One to whom creation will give an account. Remembering that Jesus became man, therefore He has to give an account until the final kingdom is in place. Jesus never fails. Consider Colossians 1:14–19:

> *14. In whom we have redemption through his blood even the forgiveness of sins:*
> *15. Who is the image of the invisible God, the firstborn of every creature:*
> *16. For by him were all things created, that are in heaven, and that are in earth, visible and invisible, whether they be thrones, or dominions, or principalities, or powers: all things were created by him, and for him:*
> *17. And he is before all things, and by him all things consist.*
> *18. And he is the head of the body, the church: who is the beginning, the firstborn from the dead; that in all things he might have the preeminence.*
> *19. For it pleased the Father that in him should all fulness dwell.*

And Colossians 2:9: *"For in him dwelleth all the fulness of the Godhead bodily."*

We can see here that man will give account. We see what Jesus did for glorified (saved) mankind. But we also see the sincerity of being on God's earth, in verse 7 in particular: *"And all kindreds of the earth shall wail because of him."* Once we reach the age of accountability, there is no excuse that will stand for us, only whether we trusted in God the Son as our Savior. The tone of the entire book is set in verse 8's words of Jesus: *"I am Alpha and Omega, the beginning and the ending, saith the Lord, which is, and which was, and which is to come, the Almighty."*

All of creation has been hurling to the moment of the actual completion of the Book of Revelation. From the creation of the angels, there has been a march to two places: those who have not reckoned with Elohim the almighty God to their doom in the lake of fire, and the righteous to the New Jerusalem. Which path are you on? The Lord Jesus Christ is about to be described in a way that was brought about by what He did in His earthly life. Has His gift of life affected you? Do you know Him as your personal Savior?

> 9. *I John, who also am your brother, and companion in tribulation, and in the kingdom and patience of Jesus Christ, was in the isle that is called Patmos, for the word of God, and for the testimony of Jesus Christ.*

John, instead of being crucified or martyred in some other way, was exiled to the isle of Patmos, where the Lord had a very special job for him to do. The last book of the Holy Bible had to be written, and who else but John the Beloved to write it. John had already been used to write four books, and the crown of prophecy was the last thing needed to give us the mind of God, the Word of God. My heart goes out to those who cannot see the Bible as God's only written word.

In verse 9, John surely says a mouthful when he says *"your brother, and companion in tribulation, and in the kingdom and patience of Jesus Christ."* The Holy Spirit instructs us about all of everyday life in these words. The brotherhood of all born-again believers is seen. We also see the tribulation and the companionship that is in this life. It is a kingdom that involves patience; it is in Jesus Christ. John being exiled and being used in the way he is about to be used exemplifies this.

> 10. *I was in the Spirit on the Lord's day, and heard behind me a great voice, as of a trumpet,*

In verse 10, John was allowed to see the images either by the Holy Spirit showing his spirit, or he was taken spiritually into heaven to observe the unfolding of this prophecy. Whichever was the case, the book was written, and the important thing is that we have it. The Holy Bible, in all of its parts, would now be complete. The Book of Revelation is the finishing touch of the revealed word of God. The love and touch of the Godhead is seen in its power and magnificence. The voice is the Lord Jesus Christ's, of course.

> *11. Saying, I am Alpha and Omega, the first and the last: and, What thou seest, write in a book, and send it unto the seven churches which are in Asia; unto Ephesus, and unto Smyrna, and unto Pergamos, and unto Thyatira, and unto Sardis, and unto Philadelphia, and unto Laodicea.*

John, in verse 11, is commissioned and commanded to write what he is about to experience. His commission comes from the One who is the first and the last of all there is; in other words, the owner of all things. The Godhead does not ask us if we would accept Him in our lives. He tells us who He is. Take it or leave it—it makes Him no difference as to His actions and His authority. What a great love that He has sent us all His Word for our help. The message is to certain churches but is to be read and cherished by all, for the Word of God is for all of mankind.

> *12. And I turned to see the voice that spake with me. And being turned, I saw seven golden candlesticks;*
> *13. And in the midst of the seven candlesticks one like unto the Son of man, clothed with a garment down to the foot, and girt about the paps with a golden girdle.*

Verse 12's candlesticks are the seven above-mentioned churches, as explained in verse 20. But quite an image is unfolding.

In verse 13, who better to write about the Lord than John the Beloved, the one who leaned on the breast, or shoulder, of the Lord at the Last Supper. It was John at the interrogation, and John at the cross, and again at the tomb; what credentials of a loving follower.

The garment and the girdle are so representative of holiness. Look where this one is standing: in the midst of the churches, if you will. Where else would the Head of the churches be? He gave His earthly life for us. Verse 14 will cement this.

14. His head and his hairs were white like wool, as white as snow; and his eyes were as a flame of fire.

The description of this One, in verse 14, is actually scary. White hair depicting age, also holiness, and then you get to the eyes—the searing, powerful, penetrating eyes of justice. Why justice, you say. The next verse will answer that for us. But keep in mind, fire is used as a purifier. These eyes show us the total sincerity and power of the One standing among the churches.

15. And his feet like unto fine brass, as if they burned in a furnace; and his voice as the sound of many waters.

Here in verse 15, we see the picture of the one metal, and the use of that metal, that describes what stands between us and a holy God. Judgment for sin, in the Old Testament tabernacle, was portrayed by brass. The feet are used because that is where we meet the road of life. The royalty and the divinity of the Lord Jesus Christ are both seen in the white robe and hair along with the golden girdle. I know that the angels have white robes; however, the entire description is of the Lord. The eyes of fire, using sight and the purifier fire, and the description of this individual is one of great power, which the Lord has already called Himself, the Almighty.

For us, applying this individually to the realm of our human life, the magnificence of this One is seen in the feet of brass. In the Book of Revelation, we will see what God portrayed with Moses and the tabernacle. Christ's feet of molten brass is a picture of the effect of the brazen altar, the cross if you will. The brazen altar was the first sacrificial place given to make atonement for sin and therefore link man and God back together. It is, in the judgment of sin, the first step in coming before a holy God. Jesus the Christ paid our sin debt as the innocent lamb and as the humble burden-bearing calf. Romans 5:11 says, *"And not only so, but we also joy in God through our Lord Jesus Christ, by whom we have now received the atonement."* This is not like the atonement of the Old Testament sacrifices, which was rollingsin's judgment forward for another year. But rather, as in John 8:36, *"If the Son therefore shall make you free, ye shall be free indeed";* and in Ephesians 1:3–7:

> 3. *Blessed be the God and Father of our Lord Jesus Christ, who hath blessed us with all spiritual blessings in heavenly places in Christ:*
> 4. *According as he hath chosen us in him before the foundation of the world, that we should be holy and without blame before him in love:*
> 5. *Having predestinated us unto the adoption of children by Jesus Christ to himself, according to the good pleasure of his will,*
> 6. *To the praise of the glory of his grace, wherein he hath made us accepted in the beloved.*
> 7. *In whom we have redemption through his blood, the forgiveness of sins, according to the riches of his grace.*

Now we know why we are called children of God and saints in the Bible.

In these verses, He boldly stands as the Almighty with the credentials to stand before the Godhead and before His eternity-bound creation. No way could any other individual be standing here in this verse—not you, not me, not an angel, not one of the so-called gods of this world, not another member of the Godhead—only the Lord Jesus Christ. If one ponders the audacity of this individual, one only needs to look at what it took for the Lord Jesus Christ to get to this point in time. Please do not forget one of the important things I just stated, that this in effect represents the brazen altar. Now, the Bible states that the Lord would only suffer once and never again. However, this picture is given to us as a reminder of what Christ did and the sincerity of God against sin and for us. The rest of the tabernacle will unfold as we go along. Interesting, isn't it?

Now, to finish the verse, we are told of the magnificent voice—not only the power of the voice, the sound of many waters, of great volume if you will, but the clarity also. There is no mistaking the sound of moving water; whether flowing like a river or falling and splashing at the bottom, you know what it is.

These verses have shown us the holiness, the antiquity, the divinity, the unquestionable power, the position and placement, and the sincerity of this individual. The Lord paid for our sins and in these verses stands as the great judge. The reason for that is He must present a holy kingdom to the Father; there is no room for sin in the kingdom.

> *16. And he had in his right hand seven stars: and out of his mouth went a sharp two-edged sword: and his countenance was as the sun shineth in his strength.*
> *17. And when I saw him, I fell at his feet as dead. And he laid his right hand upon me, saying unto me, Fear not; I am the first and the last:*

Now comes the grandeur of the judging One. In verse 16, we see the seven stars, the sharp two-edged sword, and the brilliant countenance. The glowing, brilliant One has possession and power. The seven stars are the angels of the seven churches. We see in Revelation 22:9 that God uses many of the departed saints in His working with His creation. I believe God has a guardian angel for each of us. The angels of verse 20, I believe, are these specially commissioned angels as messengers to those churches. Certainly, God doesn't have to send His angels, of whatever rank or letter. They do His bidding. We are the silly ones that need reminding and direction. He says in John, the tenth chapter, that He holds us in His hand. Most certainly, then, He holds the angels of His churches in His hand. It sure would be beneficial to us if we would follow and not try to lead God.

As for the countenance as the sun, compare, please, Daniel 10:5–8:

> *5. Then I lifted up mine eyes, and looked, and behold a certain man clothed in linen, whose loins were girded with fine gold of Uphaz:*
> *6. His body also was like the beryl and his face as the appearance of lightning, and his eyes as lamps of fire,*

10

*and his arms and his feet like in colour to polished brass,
and the voice of his words like the voice of a multitude.*

*7. And I Daniel alone saw the vision: for the men that were
with me saw not the vision; but a great quaking fell upon
them, so that they fled to hide themselves.*

*8. Therefore I was left akme, and saw this great
vision, and there remained no strength in me: for my
comeliness was turned in me into corruption, and I
retained no strength.*

John, as did Daniel, realized he had no ability to stand before
this person—no right, even as a human being, to stand before the
Holy One. Might I say to the folks who think and boast that they
will deal with God, whoever He is, when death comes their way,
look out. The only way we can stand before the awesome God
is by Him allowing it. Verse 16 leads us into John's response in
verse 17. John did the only thing he could do. In total humility
and in fear, John fell flat, because it says *"as dead."* He didn't just
go to his knees—there was no strength to stand.

Now let us look at Jesus' response. He used one of those
nail-scarred hands to touch John. Then, in reassurance, He tells
John, *"Fear not; I am the first and the last."* What a reality
for John and us; the fearsome one—yes, the one in control of
all things—*cares.* The First and the Last is the One who is the
caring One. He desires our presence; however, *on His terms.*

Jesus wants us to realize that the human Jesus was God in
a human body. He is the one who holds mankind accountable,
because He *bought* mankind. Like I said, He is by no means
lessening God the Father or God the Holy Spirit. However, He
is the one who suffered in a human body to get a particular job
done, and He will finish that job. He fully deserves this glory—
as God, yes, but also, He and He *alone* suffered the cross. Dear
one, if you do not know Him as your Savior, you and you *alone*
will suffer throughout eternity; there is no togetherness there.

*18. I am he that liveth, and was dead; and, behold, I am alive
forevermore, Amen; and have the keys of hell and of death.*

The place called hell in Luke 16:23was brought into existence as a place that was and is used as a container set apart for a particular occasion, and it has compartments. This place was used for certain fallen angels and then had to accommodate fallen man. Here in verse 18, Jesus refers back to verse 4, showing LIS that the one mentioned in verse 4 is He Himself. However, He has more to say. The Judge says, *"and have the keys of hell and of death."* Death is the meticulous accounting of and dispersal of dead mankind. I give you 1 Corinthians 15:54–58:

> *54. So when this corruptible shall have put on incorruption, and this mortal shall have put on immortality, then shall be brought to pass the saying that is written, Death is swallowed up in victory.*
>
> *55. O death, where is thy sting? O grave, where is thy victory?*
>
> *56. The sting of death is sin; and the strength of sin is the Law.*
>
> *57. But thanks be to God, which giveth us the victory through our Lord Jesus Christ.*
>
> *58. Therefore, my beloved brethren, be ye stedfast, unmoveable, always abounding in the work of the Lord, for as much as ye know that your Labour is not in vain in the Lord.*

There is no fear for those of verse 17 and of Hebrews, the fourth chapter, who are allowed to come boldly to the *throne of grace.* That throne is now, and the Lamb of God is sitting on the right side of that throne. It is the mercy seat from off the top of the ark of the tabernacle—not the earthly tabernacle, but the one that Moses was told to model the earthly tabernacle after.

The entire furniture of the tabernacle will unfold right before our eyes before this book is done. But, boy, look at those last words about the keys. The Lord holds the key of death, the power of death, yes, and the realm of death, as well as the key of hell, the grave representing hell, and especially since the Lord took captivity captive. Please don't miss the reality of the keys. I once worked at a deli, and part of my job was cooking. When I opened a box of those dead chickens and put a bag of them in the cooker, they had no choice but to be cooked. Uh-oh!

These verses of 1 Corinthians are such an encouragement to us, and this verse 18 is such a message to the lost. Please take time to be of the former and not of the latter, the lost. If you do not know the Lord Jesus Christ as your personal Savior, please accept that you are a sinner, that Jesus died on the cross to pay all sin debt, and that He is holding out salvation to you. In order to accept the gift of salvation, you must let go of self and self's ability and value. Realizing you are a sinner in much need of salvation, pray in singleness of heart to Christ, "Lord, be merciful to me, a sinner." Thank you, dear one.

The "amen" of this verse is the same thing as saying "so be it," or "let it be so." The Lord Jesus is agreeing to the first parts of the verse, and also, He is putting in motion the last parts of the verse: the payment and the fellowship with Him, and the judgment by Him that is coming. What an awesome chapter. In starting this book, I wanted to jump to chapters 4–18 because of what God had shown me. But as in all things, we must start at the beginning. I am glad I had to start at the beginning, because this is such a great chapter.

19. *Write the things which thou hast seen, and the things which are, and the things which shall be hereafter;*
20. *The mystery of the seven stars which thou sawest in my right hand, and the seven golden candlesticks. The seven stars are the angels of the seven churches: and the seven candlesticks which thou sawest are the seven churches.*

In verses 19f, John is commanded to write the things he has seen and is about to see, so the churches will have the mind of God. The seven churches—in reality, all His churches—are supposed to be submissive to Him. The Holy Spirit always blesses the spreading of the word of God. The seven stars, again, I believe these angels are departed saints with a special commission because of God dealing with His human bride. We will see this type of commission in later chapters.

Christ lives amongst and moves and rules in His body. That is what His churches are, the body of Christ. His churches are to fulfill the job that the nation of Israel did not get done. That is the spreading of the knowledge of righteousness. This chapter puts forth the magnificence and credentials of the One who is about to bring into question and scrutiny all of creation. We should already be holding our hats, but it just gets better.

Chapter 2

These next two chapters are of great importance to church history. You see, the Lord maps out how the church age is going to transpire. Keep in mind, He is not "roboting" the lives and the ages; He is just letting mankind know that He knows everything. It is strange how the individual churches and their problems and qualities could be used to show the turning of the different stages of the church age. God is awesome, isn't He? There is so much I could put into these two chapters, but, if you don't mind, we will cover what's here and keep this book a little shorter. One further point: One can also use these chapters to view the stages of om Christian life as individuals. At the close of chapter 3, we will seesome pretty revealing things about ourselves. Here we go.

1. *Unto the angel of the church of Ephesus write; These things saith he that holdeth the seven stars in his right hand, who walketh in the midst ofthe seven golden candlesticks;*
2. *I know thy works, and thy labour, and thy patience, and how thou canst not bear them which are evil: and thou hast tried them which say they are apostles, and are not, and hast found them liars:*
3. *And hast borne, and hast patience, and for my name's sake hast laboured, and hast not fainted.*
4. *Nevertheless I have somewhat against thee, because thou hast left thy first love.*
5. *Remember therefore from whence thou art fallen, and repent, and do the first works; or else I will come unto*

thee quickly, and will remove thy candlestick out of his place, except thou repent.

6. *But this thou hast, that thou hatest the deeds of the Nicolaitanes, which I also hate.*

7. *He that hath an ear, let him hear what the Spirit saith unto the churches; To him that overcometh will I give to eat of the tree of life, which is in the midst of the paradise of God*

This church has all the right things said about it; they were really awesome. Four times labor-related terminology is used, three times patience-related words, and two times their standing firm is alluded to. One thing is mentioned that sums up what they had been so busy becoming: missing the first love. The apostle John at the foot of the cross is the picture of what they lost. He watched the Lord be crucified and all the mocking, but John was faithful to the Lord. He was powerless at the trial and all the way to the cross... or was he? Even though, in John's eyes, reality vaporized before his eyes while standing there at the foot of the cross, he still trusted in the one on the cross, and His teachings. Did he understand why this was happening? Maybe he did. One thing for sure can be seen: He just kept focused on the Lord. We must stand, we must labor, we must endure. The only way to stay at peace with life is by bowing at the cross and coming boldly to the throne of grace. Amen!

The Nicolaitanes, it has been explained, is the idea and later a doctrine of "first among equals" (Rev. C. I. Scofield D. D. has a good explanation of this phrase in his works of 1909 and 1917). That is to say, we are all equal before God; however, certain ones of us are at the top of the list or should be considered before anyone else. You will find in the Book of Hebrews and in Peter's writings that we are a royal priesthood. Quite frankly, there is not one person any better than another in God's bride. Pastors and such are rightfully shown respect for the position God has put them. Can you imagine the beauty of the services if we showed proper respect to all in our services, with all of self's fleshly desires left outside and committed, loving worship inside? My friends, we will see that in the New Jerusalem.

Among the important points of chapters 2 and 3 are the instructions of overcoming. The first is seen in verse 7. Maybe it is a look at what bewildered John at the foot of the cross. He possibly realized the coming kingdom of peace. While hanging on the cross, the Lord did not look much like a tree of life. However, even though Adam rejected the Tree of Life for the fruit of rebellion, life in Christ is being nestled beside His throne. What better place to be.

He that overcomerh: Eating means fellowship, eating means tasty nourishment, eating means provision, and earing means peace. This church had all the right things said about it and its ministry, except for the following:

> a. Its fellowship was possibly still at the foot of the cross. While the cross is totally important, we must move forward to resting in the throne room of grace and living in His peace.
> b. Our nourishment must not come from an occupied cross or the bloody ground around it, but by the finished word and hope it gives.
> c. While their time of life was bitter because of being hunted and persecuted, Christ's words of *"I will be with you always"* in Matthew 28:20 should sustain us, because of His faith. I know life can totally be hard and leaning toward hopeless; however, *"the just shall live by faith"* (Rom. 1:17). Also, Philippians 4:19 says, *"But my God shall supply all your need according to his riches in glory by Christ Jesus."*
> d. While they rested on their efforts, that became their purpose. The peace of earing of the Tree of Life is that of being at peace with God, whether in His throne of grace, of Hebrews chapter 4, or grasping the love and commitment of John 14:27: *"My peace I give unto you."*

Do you sometimes find that your day is filled with doing instead of enjoying?

8. And unto the angel of the church in Smyrna write; These things saith the first and the last, which was dead, and is alive;

9. I know thy works, and tribulation, and poverty, (but thou art rich) and I know the blasphemy of them which say they are Jews, and are not, but are the synagogue of Satan.

10. Fear none of those things which thou shalt suffer: behold, the devil shall cast some of you into prison, that ye may be tried; and ye shall have tribulation ten days: be thou faithful unto death, and I will give thee a crown of life.

11. He that hath an ear, let him hear what the Spirit saith unto the churches; He that overcometh shall not be hurt of the second death.

Boy, this church had all the credentials of godliness: effort, faithfulness during trying times, and sacrifice. They are told that even more problems are coming; but there is a limit, number one, and secondly, even if the supreme sacrifice is required, God always rewards His servants. The crown of life is given to those who endure for the Lord. You see, eternity is a whole lot longer than life here on this earth, and it is glorious. This crown is given to those who choose to stand for righteousness and please the Lord instead of self or the world. That's God's way of encouraging us to endure. He endured; so should we. The last clause refreshes our memory that above all else the second death will not affect us; we can only die once, and that is in this fleshly life. We are overcomers by being in the one who overcame, *Christ.*

12. And to the angel of the church in Pergamos write; These things saith he which hath the sharp sword with two edges;

13. I know thy works, and where thou dwellest, even where Satan's seat is: and thou holdest fast my name, and hast not denied my faith, even in those days wherein Antipas was my faithful martyr, who was slain among you, where Satan dwelleth.

14. But I have a few things against thee, because thou hast there them that hold the doctrine of Balaam, who taught Balac to cast a stumblingblock before the children of Israel, to eat things sacrificed unto idols, and to commit fornication.

15. So hast thou also them that hold the doctrine of the Nicolaitanes, which thing I hate.

16. Repent; or else I will come unto thee quickly, and will fight against them with the sword of my mouth.

17. He that hath an ear, let him hear what the Spirit saith unto the churches; To him that overcometh will I give to eat of the hidden manna, and will give him a white stone, and in the stone a new name written, which no man knoweth saving he that receiveth it.

Boy, you really do not want to be in the situation of this church. Like I said, we can sometimes find these church ages in our lives, or the opportunity of these times can present themselves if we are not very careful. You know? You work and study and sacrifice and stay in the fight and sacrifice some more, and then something or someone points out a fault, a sin, or a compromise. You look at your life, hoping to see a good witness, but what you see is not what you would have described.

It's not that you left your fuse love, but rather an additional love is there also. Oops! You look around and see also that there is a place given to a thing or person or thought or a way that just will not fit, unless you make allowances for it. This is when the Word of God pulls out His two-edged sword and goes to work on you. Isn't it nice that God still cares? Our beliefs have to stand up to the Bible, and so do our lives. Keep in mind that it is our works and our fruitfulness that will suffer the scrutiny of God, not om relationship with Him. Remember, He chastises His children. Let us consider:

a. This church is told to repent and to come to a place of resolve. It was time for them to realize that they are a vessel, that the one with the two-edged sword was bringing them into judgment, and that it was time to make a decision. They can only serve one God (god) at a time.

b. Their works, their place of service, their standing fast in the faith even while one of them was martyred are not overlooked by the One in charge.

c. The Lord tells them that He has a few things against them. They are allowing the perversion of His house: the introduction of false religions, sexual perversion, and the setting up of a priesthood.

d. They are told to repent or fight against Him.

e. As in all the churches, they are urged to *hear.*

f. Overcomers have their needs provided and are assured of an eternity with God as His children.

These believers are encouraged to look inside and be strengthened and to realize a special blessing awaits them. They will have special provisions from God, and they will have a special name tag, if you will-a special emblem to hang about their neck of family origin. It is theirs alone and will be given by God Himself.

In these messages to the churches, the expression *"he that overcometh"* is used by God to encourage us as we live this life. I will finish that thought at the end of chapter 3.

18. And unto the angel of the church in Thyatira write; These things saith the Son of God, who hath his eyes like unto a flame of fire, and his feet are like fine brass;

19. I know thy works, and charity, and service, and faith, and thy patience, and thy works; and the last to be more than the first.

20. Notwithstanding I have a few things against thee, because thou sufferest that woman Jezebel, which calleth herself a prophetess, to teach and to seduce my servants to commit fornication, and to eat things sacrificed unto idols.

21. And I gave her space to repent of her fornication; and she repented not.

22. Behold, I will cast her into a bed, and them that commit adultery with her into great tribulation, except they repent of their deeds.

23. *And I will kill her children with death; and all the churches shall know that I am he which searcheth the reins and hearts: and I will give unto every one of you according to your works.*

24. *But unto you I say, and unto the rest in Ihyatira, as many as have not this doctrine, and which have not known the depths of Satan, as they speak; I will put upon you none other burden.*

25. *But that which ye have already hold fast till I come.*

26. *And he that overcometh, and keepeth my works unto the end, to him will I give power over the nations:*

27. *And he shall rule them with a rod of iron; as the vessels of a potter shall they be broken to shivers: even as I received of my Father*

28. *And I will give him the morning star.*

29. *He that hath an ear, let him hear what the Spirit saith unto the churches.*

Well, we come to a more serious situation, and no sin is small. Furthermore, neither a church nor a person wants their life taken because God had to judge to the fullest extent. But God calls the shots in all of life. These folks are being examined by the one who went through all judgment for His creation in order to pay for sin. He is now looking at them with the searing eyes of judgment and purification, with no place for them to hide. Big oops!

Not only had this church gotten too busy, maybe too tired, and too needy, but also they had gotten too easy, easy to the extent that the end justified the means. That is unacceptable in God's house, in any marriage, in any life of commitment. This church had taken the mindset of Jezebel, the wife of Ahab, to its fullest position. In verse 24, *"the depths of Satan"* is the occult. Their mindset of worshiping was to not leave God in control, but to have a group to make decisions. This church followed the mindset of Eve. We will deal with this Jezebel and the persuasion of this life in chapter 17.

What is seen in Thyatira is the mindset of mankind in general, which is seen in the book of Zechariah. The snapshot of their heart is revealed in Revelation 18:7: *"I sit a queen."*

In verse 24, God, not missing that there were some actual believers in this Jezebel, says He requires nothing else for them to enter heaven, but tells them to hold on to their faith and love their Savior. These believers are mentioned again in chapter 18. God knows our life and our circumstances. Our influence may be small, but He says to stand. Maybe our life just doesn't measure up to others or is overshadowed by others. Remember that it is God who has the eternal measuring stick that we should be concerned about.

When there is a failure in a life of commitment, there is a judgment that must follow:

a. The searing eyes of a holy God must bring judgment for willful sin. It was time for this church to pay up. God saw their works and charity and service and faith and patience and their works (again). He tells them that He knows their effort-more accurately, the kind of effort they were putting out. God can see past the effort to see the heart of those who put up a barrage of activity to hide an impure heart. They may fool the world, but not God.

b. The allowance of a false entity to be housed in God's house is unacceptable. As 1 Peter 2:9 says, all believers make up a *"royal priesthood."* God will nor stand for a Nicolaitane form in His house.

c. He gave this church and church age space to repent of this belief, which has not taken place; therefore, this will be seen in the great tribulation.

d. Those true believers are commanded to not give in to the belief

e. Those who did not give in to this belief during this church's existence would have the same position and power as any church age believer.

f. We will finish this thought with the tribulation saints of this church in chapter 18.

The last verse of this chapter expresses the mindset of a holy God: hear. God is always seeking the lost. However, the Book of Revelation shows an end of time is coming.

Chapter 3

1. And unto the angel of the church in Sardis write; These things saith he that hath the seven Spirits of God, and the seven stars; I know thy works, that thou hast a name that thou livest, and art dead.

2. Be watchful, and strengthen the things which remain, that are ready to die: for I have not found thy works perfect before God.

3. Remember therefore how thou hast received and heard, and hold fast, and repent. If therefore thou shalt not watch, I will come on thee a sa thief, and thou shalt not know what hour I will come upon thee.

4. Thou hast a few names even in Sardis which have not defiled their garments; and they shall walk with me in white: for they are worthy.

5. He that overcometh, the same shall be clothed in white raiment; and I will not blot out his name out of the book of life, but I will confess his name before my Father, and before his angels.

6. He that hath an ear, let him hear what the Spirit saith unto the churches.

These folks have to face reality; they are told that they can't hide from the searching God. All the works and prestige just don't stand up to what God knows is right. Anything for a name and a position just doesn't cut it with God. We must remember it is not our stature in this life, but our position if you will, our "knee work." When the one with the white robe and golden girdle is standing before us with those feet like burning brass and eyes like a flame, we will wish we had been purposely holy.

Now, I know that we will not reach a sinless condition this side of glory, because we are still housed in this flesh. However, we should strive to please God. We can accomplish that by giving up to Him, by not putting any evil thing before our eyes, and to go a step further, by stopping beating ourselves up. We should recognize that we already have joy, that we are sitting beside Him in His throne of grace. Please remember Hebrews 4:13ff.

Isn't it neat that in verse 5 of our text God found another way of saying we will live with Him and in grandeur?

Do we have the reality that God knows all, misses nothing, settles for only the best, closest relationship there is, and it's all for us? Really, have we put God through the wringer, so to speak? Remember, *"God so loved the world"* John 3:16). Yes, it is true. We and this church should realize this is not a game with God. Even with all the smokescreen that was in this church, God knew its heart. He knew His children and cared for them, just as in Elijah's day.

Here, the everywhere God who is in control of everything and everyone cannot sidestep, nor would He, the fact that this church exists, but He has to pronounce it dead. Of all the sacrifice it took to get it into existence, there was no power of God there. Notice there is no mention of the infiltration of the Jezebel, the Eve way, or of worship in this church. Evidently, their credentials of having come from Cluist were in place. Instead of having compromised, they replaced loving with looking. God tells them:

a. Remember, hold fast, and repent.
b. To the few believers, hold on, be watchful, strengthen.
c. If you will not, there will be sudden judgment.
d. I know you are but a few believers, but I will give you white to wear, for you are worthy.
e. I will not blot out your name, but confess it before My Father.

God knows all things.

Excessive works stem from an empty heart with knowledge that there is something missing, but with no desire to follow the given example. Sounds just like Adam, doesn't it? Consider, please, the comparison in 2 Chronicles 12:10£ Solomon's path from his house to the temple was lined on each side with golden shields. Those shields reflecting the morning sun gave an illumination on the road, whereas, as we find in the above scripture, Rehoboam's path from his house to the temple was illuminated by brass shields. Remember, brass is a type of judgment. Sin always causes us to use an imitation in order to try to uphold a former glory, if you will. Rehoboam's glory was make-believe, as was the church at Sardis.

The Thyatira church is a picture of Eve's purpose of life, one demonstrating the following attitudes:

   a. Provide for me.
   b. Enhance me.
   c. Whatever I want to do is right.
   d. Do not hold me back.

The Sardis church pictures Adam's garden reality, demonstrating these attitudes:

   a. I'm special.
   b. You owe me.
   c. What I decide is right is right.
   d. I should be able to follow my own directions.

As we have seen from the garden and the freshness of the apostles' work, one can have all the right things and opportunities and still fail.

Now let's see what God can accomplish when His people decide to do the following:

   a. Eat of the Tree of Life and not of the Tree of Knowledge of Good and Evil, as seen in Genesis 3
   b. Cling to Life, realizing there is no second death for them
   c. Trust the Provider
   d. Be ever watchful to repentance: *"Be ye holy for I am holy."*

7. *And to the angel of the church in Philadelphia write; These things saith he that is holy, he that is true, he that hath the key of David, he that openeth, and no man shutteth; and shutteth, and no man openeth;*

8. *I know thy works: behold, I have set before thee an open door, and no man can shut it: for thou hast a little strength, and hast kept my word, and hast not denied my name.*

9. *Behold, I will make them of the synagogue of Satan, which say they are Jews, and are not, but do lie; behold, I will make them to come and worship before thy feet, and to know that I have loved thee.*

10. *Because thou hast kept the word of my patience, I also will keep thee from the hour of temptation, which shall come upon all the world, to try them that dwell upon the earth.*

11. *Behold, I come quickly: hold that fast which thou hast, that no man take thy crown.*

12. *Him that overcometh will I make a pillar in the temple of my God, and he shall go no more out: and I will write upon him the name of my God, and the name of the city of my God, which is new Jerusalem, which cometh down out of heaven from my God: and I will write upon him my new name.*

13. *He that hath an ear, let him hear what the Spirit saith unto the churches.*

This church's history was good; their credentials were in place. They hadnot left their first love; they had stayed true to their Savior. This church reality is still in existence today.

Inverse 9, God wanes His creation to know that His sanctioned entity of revealing His salvation is His church. The Jewish nation that is still trying to cling to their Old Testament commission of spreading the good news of a loving God will have to come to the reality that they are not following the Son of Abraham, the Son of David, the Son of God. The last verse of Psalm 22 will be dealt with later.

What beautiful things this church is recommended for:
   a. Their works
   b. That there is some strength
   c. Their steadfastness,
   d. That they had not denied the Lord

Now that is a stand!

Well, isn't that the case with every church, you ask? Out ofseven chtuches, there were only two that were honorably mentioned. Consider that in amongst all those works, the Lord opened the verses with telling about the key of David, the kingship of the throne of Israel, the heir of Abraham. He says to this church that they have an opportunity, an open door set by God. God had a purpose (a job) for them.

I believe one of this church era's crowning moments is seen with the movement of God's people to the New World, the Americas. God's people had been so hunted by the forces of evil that when they got to the New World, they made srne that there would be religious freedom. This freedom is what made the United States great. I believe the Philadelphian age is still alive, the job that Israel had not done; that is, to give the world the opportunity to know God. This church has done and is doing this. American missionaries have spread over the world. All the churches have had that chance. Putting forth a true message of the kingdom of God for a lost and dying world has been God's purpose all along.

Verse 10 speaks of the church being protected from the hour of temptation, the tribulation. This is the calling out of all believers as seen in I Thessalonians 4:13ff.

Verse 11 mentions the opportunity of us losing our crowns. We have rewards waiting on us because of loving the Lord and serving Him. We have crowns set up for us, but these can be abolished if we faint in our service—that is to say, we weaken our stand and resolve against sin.

The Lord has been telling these churches tocontinue to stand. We can never lose our position because it's His hand we are in, not His in ours. To fail is one thing, but to commit to fail is another. To die in battle is a tragedy; however, to help the enemy get a victory is something altogether different. For a born-again believer in the Lord Jesus Christ, to die is graduation time. We will be home one day. Amen.

Verse 12 tells us of the coming kingdom and the reality of belonging. Remember, we overcome only because He is the overcomer whom we are in. We fail because we try to lead and decide (an Eve attitude) instead of walk and follow (an Abraham attitude). I know it seems like we are going through a tough life. Admittedly, there are hard times, but ours is Christ's life, since we are dead to self and alive in Christ.

This precious church is reminded of the example that they follow, of His strength and ability and His certain purpose. They are urged not to faint, but to be like one of the magnificent pillars of Solomon's temple. What a presence those two pillars were, and they were given names. We shall be given special names too. Christ will havea new name and we will too. lhink ofit- God's family name. A-a-a-a-men!

One last thought about this church is the very thing that Jesus showed to all. The Lord said to love one another. The apostle John, in 1John 4:8, said that God is love and we should love one another. Love for souls, as commanded by our Lord, has been its driving force, along with a committed love for God. This is what set this church apart from all the rest, and still does.

The Laodicean church stands for a reality check. But let us look first at God's "reality" comments about His creation, before and after the flood. Genesis 6:5 says, *"And God saw that the wickedness of man was great in the earth, and that every imagination of the thoughts of his heart was only evil continually"*; and Jeremiah 17:9 concurs: *"The heart is deceitful above all things, and desperately wicked: who can know it?"*

> *14. And unto the angel of the church of the Laodiceans write; These things saith the Amen, the faithful and true witness, the beginning of the creation of God;*
> *15. I know thy works, that thou art neither cold nor hot: I would thou wert cold or hot.*

16. So then because thou art lukewarm, and neither cold nor hot, I will spue thee out of my mouth.

17. Because thou sayest, I am rich, and increased with goods, and have need of nothing; and knowest not that thou art wretched, and miserable, and poor, and blind, and naked:

18. I counsel thee to buy of me gold tried in the fire, that thou mayest be rich; and white raiment, that thou mayest be clothed, and that the shame of thy nakedness do not appear; and anoint thine eyes with eyesalve, that thou mayest see.

19. As many as I love, I rebuke and chasten: be zealous therefore, and repent.

The question comes up, Are these last two churches blended together in these times in which we live? Is there a coming wimpy church age? Could there be a feathering effect taking place between the Philadelphian church age and the Laodicean church age?

No! The Philadelphian church age is an ongoing church reality. Now, is there a washing away of the stand of many churches? Yes, but God promised He would always have a witness. Many times in His Word, He says He raises up and tears down. The beautiful Ephesian church was a good example of God not pulling punches. They had to face the reality of God saying, "Walk with Me, or I will judge you."

I have to insert something here. While God does see past the outside to the heart, this attitude of coming to God's house in any apparel is okay teaches a false doctrine of as long as you come to God's house, that is all that matters, as is seen in many churches today. It is true our best is good enough for God, but we do not have the right to display ro Him a "take it or leave it" attitude.

The Laodicean church is God's perfect example of people playing church, or to put it another way, man trying to soothe his need to worship, to feel good about himself. They needed to be satisfied with their look. They did not care about the purpose of the church. They had it made, in their minds, and that was all that was important.

The Laodicean church is the perfect picture of Adam's attitude in the garden:

a. He was willing to go along.
b. He was willing to disobey.
c. He didn't want to stand on his own two feet.
d. Even though he knew God, and that everyt.hing came from God, and that God had said to multiply, he was content to take it easy in a cushy place.

They had heard the gospel, but the main thing was to satisfy themselves.

God tells them to buy gold that has been tried in the fire, salvation—to move from self to committed belief Salvation has none of us or our abilities in its reality, only our accepting His gift of salvation by faith. He was telling them to put their treasures in heaven, not on earth; that is, to stop thinking they were really something when all we are is putrefying flesh. They could have white raiment, which is the righteousness of commitment to God. God sees past our veils of smokescreens.

The eye salve is tears of repentance washing away the willingness to see what we want to see and not what is actually there to see, to see ourselves as we really are: needy, helpless, worthless in the eyes of eternity. Anything less than Christ in our lives is failure, or to put it another way, to not be His child.

When the Lord says that He stands at the door and knocks, He is letting us know that He will not share His throne in our hearts with anyone or anything else. This church did not know Christ as their Savior; their desire was the show. Do we want victory and His presence?

One could say that the Laodicean church is the evolutionary end of the path that started in Ephesus, went through Pergamos, and is gasping in the death of Sardis. It is characterized by the following:

a. No strength
b. No shame
c. No reality
d. No humility

e. No vision

f. No desire

g. And last of all, no presence

This church is the finality of the results of Eve's attitude and Adam's reality, grand in their thought, miserable in their existence. Adam and Eve were cast our, and this church was spewed out. Adam and Eve's garden reality was one of unbelief, as is seen in the Laodicean church.

God could only say that there was an opportunity to have honor by turning from self to God. In so doing, they would have rewards in heaven and beautiful white garments instead of shame. They would have a clear vision of life here and of heaven. God is always holding out an invitation.

The results of Eve's sin are easily seen in the Laodicean church. They were spewed out by God, and Adam and Eve were cast out by God. God clothed Adam and Eve with animal skins, showing the way of worship had a cost. The Laodicean church is told that there is a cost for them to be able to worship.

Thecost of Adam's "go along" attitude is seen in all the world. Adam should have stood for God and righteousness instead of being led by a woman, as is seen in Thyatira. Now let's summarize the churches and Adam:

1. Ephesus: Adam left his first love (God); he knew where Eve got the fruit.
2. Smyrna: He was faced with temptation, and God had already told him about death.
3. Pergamos: Adam chose Eve and the fruit.
4. Thyatira: Adam clung to sin instead of God. Adam and Eve had to be judged.
5. Sardis: Adam was dead (separated from God).
6. Philadelphia: God provided for Adam.
7. Laodicea: Adam's descendants are born in shame (naked) and in sin.

Now let's turn the coin over:

1. Ephesus: Adam could have had the Tree of Life and lived in peace.
2. Smyrna: There would have been no death.
3. Pergamos: Adam would have had provision and closeness.
4. Thyatira: Adam would have had power and God's presence.
5. Sardis: Adam would have had his righteousness proclaimed before the Father.
6. Philadelphia: Adam would have remained a pillar ofcreation.
7. Laodicea: Adam would have remained for the glory of God; he would have had no sin, hence no shame. He could have enjoyed the garden.

The last three verses of chapter 3 are some of the most familiar verses of the Bible. I think they belong to the verses about the church of Laodicea. However, they are usable for all of us because the Lord knocks at all hearts and must be let in to live and love. Will we be selfish, conceited, and lazy, or will we see the need to turn, and in love, serve?

Let me state something here. Paul stressed many times to guard the house of God. I find, as in his day, that the wolves of Satan have crept in and are most brutal. One other thing: These people who go around slapping people on the head or wherever and claim the person to be healed, I watch with my good eye. One must follow God's Word for God's results. The Lord in the Gospels and the Book of James tells us how to do that. All those who practice a show of works outside the Word of God do not have God's blessing. I do, however, believe in healing faith.

The encouragement given to each of these churches belongs to born-again believers throughout all the ages. The promises of sitting, eating, belonging, and of ruling are ours.

God's purpose for the churches of these chapters is for our instruction to guard and win, for, you see, what comes next is brutal.

The seven churches do give the history of what is going to happen (did happen) in the churches. To finish about the churches, we need to consider the following:

1. Ephesus had no real power, love if you will, no driving desire for the Lord. Hence, they had no world-changing fruit. We see this same thing in some religious efforts today.

2. Smyrna's example is that they gave up. They had all the right stuff but quit. Aren't we glad that the Lord did not quit?

3. Pergamos chose their own authority, their own name, their own credentials, their own provisions. This is exemplified in the nondenominational names of those church groups that have come along but cannot trace their heritage back to before the cross. Author's note: Christ had his church while he walked with them on a daily basis and had a treasurer, Judas.

4. Thyatira shows the system mixture of idolatry and Christianity.

5. Sardis shows the heritage but has no godly desire to accomplish anything that has the hand of God in it. Evangelism of the world is not an option.

6. Philadelphia has the right heritage, the love, the desire, the right effort. It is the picture of the early churches that were started by those sent out to start new churches. The churches that came from Jerusalem and stayed true the teaching of the Lord and the guidance of the Holy Spirit, saw a very bloody time, especially in the dark ages. We can see their heritage still today. To start on a journey into church history, first use the small book by James Milton Carroll called "The Trail of Blood".

7. Laodicea is the "easy believism" result of self-willed worship, which is so prevalent today; that is, just please self. Change, as is necessary, to make oneself happy. Call on God. Call on Jesus. All the while, there is no concept of the true and living God.

34

20. Behold, I stand at the door, and knock: if; any man hear my voice, and open the door, I will come in to him, and will sup with him, and he with me.

21. To him that overcometh will Igrant to sit with mein my throne, even as I also overcame, and am set down with my Father in his throne.

Jesus' role as creator, leader, teacher, guide, and savior is seen in the last three verses:

1. He desires that we live with Him.
2. He will give us life with Him.
3. His promise is to live with us and us with Him, hence with the Father.

Verse 22 is the last time the church is mentioned in the Book of Revelation.

Chapter 4

1. After this I looked, and, behold, a door was opened in heaven: and the first voice which I heard was as it were of a trumpet talking with me; which said, Come up hither, and I will shew thee things which must be hereafter.

Okay, now we are to the part that has made my head spin with questions. Please be patient with me and you will see the tabernacle unfold. Also, you will see the tribulation in its segments and the glory of God as full as this meager boy can get it. I need to make a point first.

The church is not mentioned from this point. The church age people are taken out just before this era starts because we are in Christ, and Christ can never be judged again (Heb. 9:26). Now, *that's* neat, and oh boy, I am glad!

In verse 1, the magnificent voice of chapter 1 is used again there is a calling to come up hither. Though this is to the apostle John, it is symbolic of the church age people, dead and alive, being called out and into heaven. The church is not mentioned again in the Bible. This is the fulfilling of 1 Thessalonians 4:16f

At this place in the Book of Revelation, the attention of the book goes from earth to heaven. The Lord has ended His work of revealing righteousness and showing grace. He has taken out the living saved saints and the bodies of the dead saints. Anything that has to do with God's effort to show Himself to His creation is removed.

Mankind begins a new era, a chance to prove itself, if you will. I will finish this thought later, but there is a reason for the segments. As we will see, there will be some witnesses established. But the world will have to come to grips with the fact that millions of its population have vanished. It will have to come to grips with the reality that the Holy Spirit is no longer on this earth as He was with the purpose of the church age.

> *2. And immediately I was in the spirit: and, behold, a throne was set in heaven, and one sat on the throne.*
> *3. And he that sat was to look upon like a jasper and a sardine stone: and there was a rainbow round about the throne, in sight like unto an emerald.*

In verses 2f, the color of the One on the throne (God the Father) is described as red-orange, with a variety of other colors that could be present, in particular green. The visage is one of clearness, of a certain clarity, but not transparent or emitting an extensive amount of light. Webster's dictionary also indicates that there probably was not a variety of individual light rays emitted or reflected. The mind does spin with what God the Father will actually look like when we get to see Him.

What is the deal with the situation of this throne? The Gospel of John says that God is light. Jesus said that He is the Light of the World in John 8:12. Yet the one on this throne is not giving out very much light, and what is seen is an image of darker colors. I think there are two reasons for this:

1. The job of the One on this throne is to bring judgment, not salvation. The exuberance of His love is engulfed in the judgment of sin.

I beheld till the thrones were cast down, and the Ancient of days did sit, whose garment was white as snow, and the hair of his head like the pure woof: his throne was like the fiery flame, and his wheels as burning fire. A fiery steam issued and came forth from before him: thousand thousands ministered unto him, and ten thousand times

ten thousand stood before him: the judgment was set, and
the books were opened. (Dan. 7:9–10)

2. If He let Himself be seen in His brilliance, nothing else
   could be seen, and God wants us to see all that is present.
   The reality, the sincerity, and the commitment of this
   throne must not be missed. The loving and giving God
   sat on the other thrones, but not on this throne.

The throne has a rainbow round about it. Even though the
Lord is cloaking Himself, there is still a brilliance of beauty about
Him, still noting that it is dark in color. May I interject here, can we
imagine what God's throne looked like before Lucifer fell, him
being covered in jewels and being the covering cherub? When
God does something, He does it right. One other thought: What
about His presence in our lives, in salvation, and in eternity? The
same God does it right; that is why we should be the happiest
people and should be sharing that hope.

4. *And round about the throne were four and twenty seats:*
   and upon the seats I saw four and twenty elders sitting,
   clothed in white raiment; and they had on their heads
   crowns of gold.

At the calling out of the church, it is sudden and it is total.
The Old Testament saints will also be with the Lord when He
comes to get us. Remember, the Lord took the saints out of
Abraham's bosom when He rose, but there is no mention of
them receiving glorified bodies. They will be with the Lord to
receive their glorified bodies, just like the dead New Testament
saints. That is why there are twenty-four elders on these sears,
twelve from each testament.

In these verses, a throne is displayed in all its beauty. But
which throne is it? In the Old Testament, the mercy seat was
atop the ark, fashioned after the one in heaven. Could this be
the mercy seat? No, the mercy seat was for the Old Testament
time period. In the Book of Revelation, you will not find mercy.

Is it the throne of grace? No, the throne of grace is where God the Father and God the Lord Jesus Christ are today.

Take a look at Hebrews 4:14–16:

> *14. Seeing then that we have a great high priest, that is passed into the heavens, Jesus the Son of God, let us hold fast our profession.*
> *15. For we have not an high priest which cannot be touched with the feeling of our infirmities; but was in all points tempted like as we are, yet without sin.*
> *16. Let us therefore come boldly unto the throne of grace, that we may obtain mercy, and find grace to help in time of need.*

Could this be the judgment seat of Christ? No. Though not mentioned in verse 1 of this chapter, the judgment seat of Christ rakes place at the calling out of the church. What happens at that judgment sear is the purifying of the works of each of the faithful. From Adam to the last person to get saved just before Christ comes to take out the church, their works are judged by the consuming fire of holiness. What remains is the reward of the faithful, their crowns.

I know it is strange to think of the Old and NewTestament saints at the judgment seat of Christ, but hold on. They all are in Christ. Give me time, because it will fall into place.

> *11. For other foundation can no man lay than that is laid, which is Jesus Christ.*
> *12. Now if any man build upon this foundation gold, silver, precious stones, wood, hay, stubble;*
> *13. Every man's work shall be made manifest: for the day shall declare it, because it shall be revealed by fire; and the fire shall try every man's work of what sort it is.*
> *14. If any man's work abide which he hath built thereupon, he shall receive a reward.*
> *15. If any man's work shall be burned, he shall suffer loss: but he himself shall be saved, yet so as by fire.*
>
> —1 Corinthians 3:11–15

What I just stated about the judgment seat of Christ is not the normal teaching about this seat. But certain things just did not add up, so please hear me out. I am not a Vulcan, or Star Trek person, but God is logical. And why nor? We will see He knew everything about creation before He created, so should He be surprised about something and act illogically?

If God's throne is going to be encircled by twelve elders of the Old Testament and twelve elders from the New Testament, all on thrones and each with at least one crown, then He will have to give them their glorified bodies at the time of the calling out; in other words, the occasion of 1 Thessalonians, chapter 4. These elders also represent the culmination of God's creation; that is, adoring mankind.

There is a question about this throne that I will answer later just to see if you pick up on it. It is a very important event.

The throne in chapter 4 is God's throne of righteousness. This throne depicts the three Godhead members in their roles and in our lives individually, as shown in God's Word. It is their opportunity to judge sin to the fullest and rid their creation of it.

God the Father is present because He is everywhere. The seven lamps of fire are the Holy Spirit, but also because of Christ's words in the Gospel of John 14:23 that He and the Father would come and dwell with us, and that He is in the Father and the Father is in Him. Also, what we have already seen in Colossians is that the fullness of the Godhead dwells in Christ. However, God the Father is not mentioned by name. This scene is the setting right of God's creation, the getting rid of sin, if you will.

The splendor, the unparalleled beauty, and the extreme brilliance are easy to see in God's Word, and logical to imagine. Its true depths of beauty we will realize in heaven. The structure of the room, or area, is this: there is a center focal point, and there are entities around the center. In verses 3-5, we see God the Son, His brilliance, His grandeur, subdued yet still unmistakable. We are then pointed to the outer circle, if you will, and see an encircling of elders, presumably and assuredly twelve from each of the testaments, all representing adoring mankind. We must move on.

Do you remember, I mentioned that the tabernacle would unfold right before our eyes?

    a. Christ is the door, *"Come up hither."* Christ said in John 14, *"I am the way."* His life, His flesh, the veil if you will, He Himself is the only way to enjoy heaven.

    b. The cross has taken place; if you will, the brazen altar of the tabernacle, Jesus enduring our judgment of sin. We will come back to this.

Now comes the results of the mindset of ignoring the brazen altar, the cross.

> *5. And out of the throne proceeded lightnings and thunderings and voices: and there were seven lamps of fire burning before the throne, which are the seven spirits of God.*

The first part of verse 5 shows movement from the general overview of the throne to the general attitude of the throne. This being the throne of righteousness means the following:

    a. Lightnings: There are judgments going out.

    b. Thunderings: These are God's proclamations against sin.

    c. Voices: These are acclamations of righteous behavior, righteous judgments, if you will.

The second part of verse 5 moves us from the outer edge of the throne to the presence of the Holy Spirit in the throne. This is the lampstand in the Holy Place of the temple. The lamps represent the power of the Holy Spirit; the number seven represents His full attention. Being equal to the other two members of the Godhead, of course He has to be here. All the Godhead seeks the end of sin. In the Bible, the Holy Spirit never seeks to glorify Himself, and the Lord Jesus is the one who suffered in a fleshly form. However, in the third chapter of Mark, the Lord has some very stern words about those who would slight the Holy Spirit.

Now, let's get caught up with the parts of the tabernacle; the same applies to the temple. In fact, what Moses was told to build was fashioned after the temple in heaven.

Remember John 10:7, where the Lord says, *"I am the door."* The temple had a door and a veil; these represented the Lord Jesus taking on human flesh. Just inside the entry there was the brazen altar, which represented the place of the judgment of sin. The sacrifices were consumed by fire. Oh, dear one, consider that all those young cattle and other animals that were offered on the altar as burnt offerings pictured the Lord Jesus in the agony of the cross. They had already died, but He had to endure all of Psalm 22. Lord, I am sorry.

What could the brazen altar be but a picture of the cross and the Lord Jesus going into hell for us? But praise God, it could not keep Him. The Book of Hebrews says that He became sin for us. Revelation 1's description of the Lord having feet like molten brass represents the Lord taking our place in the judgment of sin. That sure is an awesome love, now isn't it?

That job is finished. That is why you will not find the brazen altar in the Book of Revelation. As the Book of Hebrews says, there is no more sacrifice for sin; hence, there is no other need of a place for a sacrifice.

6. And before the throne there was a sea of glass like unto crystal

I separated this part because I wanted to deal with it separately. The laver in Solomon's temple was also called a sea. It was vast and beautifully built. Please note that it is referred to here as *"like unto crystal."* The water is calm, at this point, in this sea.

Remember, the tribulation is just getting started. Observe the laver's position and purpose in the tabernacle and temple; it is after the cross. It is not part of salvation; it is the result of salvation: *"But the water that I shall give him shall be in him a well of water springing up into everlasting life"* (John 4:14).

The laver was a big water basin. In the Gospel of John, the Lord is called the water of life. Please picture what the Lord is

42

saying here. The approach to God is through the door. Sin has been judged, and the next thing you see is the water of life. In symbolism, water represents life, or the ability of living. I will finish this thought in the last chapter. But think of the picture of the sacrifices taking place in the tabernacle and the temple. Picture the great laver receiving water and water being taken out for washing and for filling the smaller lavers.

Please picture the ground wet with blood around the brazen altar of the Old Testament from all the blood of the sacrifices, as stated in Leviticus 4:7. The ground around the laver was wet with water from the transferring of water for washing.

One seeking God must do the following:

    a. One must enter His door.
    b. The blood must beapplied: "We have redemption through his blood" (Col. 1:14).
    c. That person will receive His water of life–all before he/she can come boldly into the throne of grace.

Now we will use verses 6–8 for the rest of the tabernacle.

> *6. And before the throne there was a sea of glass like unto crystal: and in the midst of the throne, and round about the throne, were four beasts full of eyes before and behind.*
> *7. And the first beast was like a lion, and the second beast like a calf, and the third beast had a face as a man, and the fourth beast was like a flying eagle.*
> *8. And the four beasts had each of them six wings about him; and they were full of eyes within: and they rest not day and night, saying, Holy, holy, holy, Lord God Almighty, which was, and is, and is to come._*

In verses 6–8, we have already dealt with the laver; however, the rest of these verses reveal some very interesting information about this throne. We already have a throne encircled twice, and then verse 6 says *"and in the midst of the throne and round about*

43

the throne. " Each one of these beasts displays a facet of Christ's earthly life.

Finishing verse 6, we see that the beasts were full of eyes, this representing the all-seeing God, the omnipresent God; if you will, Jesus.

In verse 7, the first beast, being the lion, is representing the Lion of the tribe of Judah; this is ownership of the throne of David. However, the majesty of the Lord is also seen, along with great strength, cunning, and veracity. He is the lawgiver.

Next is seen the calf, which points to the atonement-bearing sacrifice of the Lord, the burden-bearer. He carried our sins on the cross.

The third beast is, of course, as a man, the earthly ministry of our Savior. There had to be a holy human sacrifice to atone for our sins.

Lastly, the eagle represents speed, beauty, again majesty, but even more, the eagle is flying. If I remember correctly, Bobby Thompson, who I think was from one of the Carolinas and was an evangelist, had five eagle messages. My friends, I would love to have those messages; they are totally awesome. He explains that the flying eagle (now, I was listening to a tape, so I'm guessing here) has its claws out, like it's always ready to grab. That does represent justice, and also, He's always ready to grab on to us to help us, to save us. The Lord is always ready, willing, and able to help us.

If you ever get a chance to get those messages, they will truly bless your heart. Also, they are extremely informative of the God given abilities of the eagle. I would love to have a set.

Now we reach verse 8. The six wings correspond with the number of man, being created on the sixth day, and the Lord did become man. The eyes mentioned would be the all-seeing ability of the Lord Jesus. He is all-knowing, all-powerful, and all-present, or everywhere, in other words.

Remembering that this is the throne of righteousness, one should easily see that the all-present Lord Jesus can be in the center of the throne and still be represented in His other jobs also.

In verse 8, we read, *"Holy, holy, holy, Lord God Almighty, which was, and is, and is to come,"* which, of course, is speaking of the Lord Jesus, using the description from chapter 1.

The throne of righteousness is the Godhead bringing a righteous end to sin and establishing a glorified kingdom in which to enjoy His creation. That, my friends, is the purpose of this throne.

Let me point out something usually missed about these four beasts:

1. The lion is the candlestick—the light-giver, the law-giver, the path-giver.
2. The calf is the golden altar—the burden of sin-bearer, a sweet savor.
3. The man is the table of shewbread—the bread of life.
4. The eagle is the mercy seat—the soaring majesty of holiness. The mercy seat rested on top of the word of God. The eagle has five lenses in its eye and can easily fly toward the sun if other birds of prey pursue it. It can look at the sun and not be harmed; the other birds cannot. That is what Bobby Thomson said in his eagle tapes.

In those four things, do you see the Lord Jesus?
Have you ever seen the temple described like this? Neither had I.

9. And when those beasts give glory and honour and thanks to him that sat on the throne, who liveth for ever and ever,
10. The four and twenty elders fall down before him that sat on the throne, and worship him that liveth for ever and ever, and cast their crowns before the throne, saying,
11. Thou art worthy, O Lord, to receive glory and honour and power: for thou hast created all things, and for thy pleasure they are and were created._

Here in verses 9ff, we see the beasts and the elders giving glory, honor, and thanks to the one on the throne. The beasts did not fall down. Did you notice the casting of the crowns of the elders? The throne of righteousness is the opening scene of the ending of the judgment for sin. God has to finish the chosen path of His creation.

This is the adoration of mankind of a holy God. It must incorporate the Lord Jesus Christ, the humble Adam. Mankind had to have a Father figure, and sin had to be judged. All had to be done with righteousness, not compromise. This is a beautiful chapter, and we should now have fewer questions pop up.

Chapter 5

The seals are the seals of indictment associated with God's criminal judgment. They are the outline of the judgment pronounced.

> *1. And I saw in the right hand of him that sat on the throne a book written within and on the backside, sealed with seven seals.*
> *2. And I saw a strong angel proclaiming with a loud voice, Who is worthy to open the book, and to loose the seals thereof?*
> *3. And no man in heaven, nor in earth, neither under the earth, was able to open the book, neither to look thereon.*
> *4. And I wept much, because no man was found worthy to open and to read the book, neither to look thereon.*

Both the book in the hand of the Father on the throne and the book mentioned in Daniel 7:9f detail theend times and speak of great tribulation. Both are sealed under authority of God. God has plenty to say about evil and the eradication of it; we will see this later. Not a wimpy, but a strong angel is in charge of finding someone to open the book. I really don't think there is a wimpy angel, but a strong angel is mentioned. You see, an angel cannot open the book; it can only be opened by a man.

No man anywhere was able to open the book or to look upon it. Why, you ask, does it have to be a man? The book pertains to mankind. The angels made their choice when Lucifer fell; angels don't need books. Then was created mankind. Mankind fell, and by man there must be a bridge made between God and man. Jesus was born to pay the debt that unjust man could not pay.

There was not found a man either in heaven, or living on the earth, or one who had gone to hell that was able to even look upon the book. We were created in God's image, but we just do not stack up to the requirements needed for that job. Adam, just like us, made badchoices. You say, "Well, Jesus was a man." Yes, but He was holy in all aspects of life. Why is this scene so dramatic then? Keep in mind what we have witnessed about the throne and the four beasts. Remember that the job of bringing about a righteous creation must be completed.

> 5. And one of the elders saith unto me, Weep not: behold, the Lion of the tribe of Judah, the Root of David, hath prevailed to open the book, and to loose the seven seals thereof
>
> 6. And I beheld, and, lo, in the midst of the throne and of the four beasts, and in the midst of the elders, stood a Lamb as it had been slain, having seven horns and seven eyes, which are the seven Spirits of God sent forth into all the earth.
>
> 7. And he came and took the book out of the right hand of him that sat upon the throne.

These verses speak of the Lion, and the Root of David, and the sacrificed Lamb that is alive and has certain features. You ask *why.*

When the Lord comes on the scene as represented by the two beasts, the Lion and the Root of David (Man), it is not in an iffy situation. We must see that God does not give leeway to what man thinks. What God is going to do, He is going to do; and no one is going to change that.

You know, that sure is nice, because we always mess things up. Now, aren't you glad God does not put any stock in humans' ability, when it comes to salvation and our daily lives? Now, how does Jesus, the Savior of mankind, come on the scene?

He comes as a sacrificed lamb, but much more. He shows He has met the demands of the Godhead for a pure, proper sacrifice. He shows His authority with the seven horns, meaning complete authority. He further shows the anointing of the Holy Spirit: the seven eyes. The Lord must be depicted in this manner. Notice, please, this image does not show up as one of the beasts. It is an image of suffering. The beasts do not represent weakness or frailty or injury. Just a reminder here—the Lord will not suffer twice.

In verse 7, He comes with confidence and takes the book, fully representative of what He is: truly of the earth, but much more. He was hmnble man, and yet still is great God. The moment in time that this verse takes place is some kind of moment—the crown of creation and the authority of God. Wow! Let's go on.

> 8. And when he had taken the book, the four beasts and four and twenty elders fell down before the Lamb, having every one of them harps, and golden vials full of odours, which are the prayers of saints.
> 9. And they sung a new song, saying, Thou art worthy to take the book, and to open the seals thereof: for thou wast slain, and hast redeemed us to God by thy blood out of every kindred, and tongue, and people, and nation;
> 10. And hast made us unto our God kings and priests: and we shall reign on the earth.

Now you say, "Aha, why are the beasts falling down?" That is a good question. Here again, the throne is here for righteousness and to finish creation's need of judgment of sin. these four will not be seen in the last throne. Also seen is the crucified Lamb. The beasts show the characteristics of the one on the throne. The Lamb shows the means by which God made justification possible for mankind. The four beasts represent what it rook to get to this point of the Lamb and the bringing of an end to the turmoil we brought into God's creation.

Between the center seat and the twenty-four elders, there is a mankind Personage and the Mover or Empowerer. The authority of this Lamb is unquestioned, even by the one on the center seat of the throne.

The harps represent pleasant living, adoration, etc. Notice, they are not holding swords. And isn't it neat that our prayers are special to God and are put into golden vials, number one? But look, they are kept. Stop and think with me of all the times you have prayed the same old prayers. I'm not talking about read prayers; I'm talking about earnest, heartfelt prayers that we just keep asking for certain needs for others as well as for ourselves. Do you remember thinking that nothing ever happens? Well, God does not overlook anything. God does care.

Okay, now let's look at the song of verse 9. This is a song of happened reality. What I mean is the earthly life of God's people is over and they are in heaven. Keep in mind the time frame here. God has finished one time and is instituting another, judgment for sin and finishing His kingdom.

The point is we have a Redeemer. People from all over the globe will be here appreciating that the Lamb has made it possible for us to be kings and priests, and that we will reign on earth. I am the most unworthy nobody there has ever been, and yet the Lamb is able to make even me worthy to reign.

> *11. And I beheld, and I heard the voice of many angels round about the throne and the beasts and the elders: and the number of them was ten thousand times ten thousand, and thousands of thousands;*
> *12. Saying with a loud voice, Worthy is the Lamb that was slain to receive power, and riches, and wisdom, and strength, honour, and glory, and blessing.*

God uses this opportunity to include all of heaven to show the proper adoration of the Lamb. You notice the Father was not included, because He is still the designated one to whom the Lamb answers.

> *13. And every creature which is in heaven, and on the earth, and under the earth, and such as are in the sea, and all that are in them, heard I saying, Blessing, and honour, and glory, and power, be unto him that sitteth upon the throne, and unto the Lamb for ever and ever.*
> *14. And the four beasts said, Amen. And the four and twenty elders fell down and worshipped him that liveth for ever and ever.*

To these verses I interject Genesis 3:17–19:_

> *17. And unto Adam he said, Because thou hast hearkened unto the voice of thy wife, and hast eaten of the tree, of which I commanded thee, saying, Thou shalt not eat of it: cursed is the ground for thy sake; in sorrow shalt thou eat of it all the days of thy life;*
>
> *18. Thorns alsoand thistles shall it bringforth to thee; and thou shalt eat the herb of the field;*
>
> *19. In the sweat of thy face shalt thou eat bread, till thou return unto the ground; for out of it wast thou taken:for dust thou art, and unto dust shalt thou return.*

And Romans 8:18–23:_

> *18. For I reckon that the sufferings of this present time are not worthy to be compared with theglory which shall be revealed in us.*
>
> *19. For the earnest expectation of the creature waiteth for the manifestation of the sons of God.*
>
> *20. For the creature was made subject to vanity, not willingly, but by reason ofhim who hath subjected the same in hope,*
>
> *21. Because the creature itself also shall be delivered from the bondage of corruption into the glorious liberty of the children of God.*
>
> *22. For we know that the whole creation groaneth and travaileth in pain together until now.*
>
> *23. And not only they, but ourselves also, which have the first fruits of the Spirit, even we ourselves groan within ourselves, waiting for the adoption, to wit, the redemption of our body.*

God's creation desires to be free of the curse of Genesis 3 and to be at peace with its creator. The Lord said in the Gospels that all of creation honors God except for man; however, here we see all of creation has a chance to glorify God.

Do we really grasp the humbling sense of what will be happening? Other than the ungodly mankind still on earth, there will be such an occasion of praise that has not happened since Adam fell. You know, that should display to us the patience of God to wait till this moment to have His proper acknowledgment. Please note that the beasts say amen; they do not fall down and worship because they, He, and the Lamb were also mentioned in this adoration.

Chapter 6

Now, folks, we get to the outline that I think has never been seen before. I know that I have never seen this outline in all the times of reading Revelation. I have neither read nor heard anyone express this outline. But finally, God got me to understand the answers to the questions that just kept nagging at me. I hope I can express these answers properly.

Chapter 6 is the outline of the sequences of God's tribulation judgment against mankind.

As you can see with my illustration, the seals come off in the form of the outline so God can open the book and bring forth the judgments. I've never seen this sequence before.

In order for God to fulfill the sealed Book of Daniel, He has to open the seals. Seals 1–6 give the outline, or table of contents, if you will. Seal 7 allows the book to open and exposes the trumpets and vials that God did not want seen in the Old Testament time. Only when the last seal is broken will God begin judging. As Daniel 11:36 says, *"For that that is determined shall be done."* Oh, my friend! Satan and mankind think they can do things their way. But God says, "I don't think so."

> *1. And I saw when the Lamb opened one of the seals, and I heard, as it were the noise of thunder, one of the four beasts saying, Come and see.*
> *2. And I saw, and behold a white horse: and he that sat on him had a bow; and a crown was given unto him: and he went forth conquering, and to conquer.*

The man that is first on the scene will end up with great power. But we must realize he gets this position by already having a demon. That demon will make his audience attentive to his words. They will already have a great desire for a special leader.

This is the first half of the tribulation. Mankind is left to itself, except for 144,000 witnesses, which will have a centrally located ministry. There will be two other witnesses; these will be discussed later. I believe that Michael and his angels have battled Satan and his angels and placed them in the bottomless pit. This will be dealt with more thoroughly in chapters 9, 12, and 17.

God's design is to prove a point, just like the point of the thousand-year reign: man is evil continually. This occasion is to show the path of man without any evil influence. The first thing we see is that of a conquering attitude, Nimrod's attitude, as the theme of the day. This mindset is always the case with mankind, along with *"evil continually"* (Gen. 6:5) as is stated by God in Noah's day.

> *3. And when he had opened the second seal, I heard the second beast say, Come and see.*
> *4. And there went out another horse that was red:and power was given to him that sat thereon to take peace from the earth, and that they should kill one another: and there was given unto him a great sword.*

This is the start of the second half of the tribulation. Notice the introduction of red, indicating peace is taken from the earth, killing is encouraged, and lastly a great sword is given. The sword certainly means death to follow. Keep in mind the sword for later.

> *5. And when he had opened the third seal, I heard the third beast say, Come and see. And I beheld, and lo a black horse; and het hat sat on him had a pair of balances in his hand.*
> *6. And I heard a voice in the midst of the four beasts say, A measure of wheat for a penny, and three measures of barley for a penny; and see thou hurt not the oil and the wine.*
> *7. And when he had opened the fourth seal, I heard the voice of the fourth beast say, Come and see.*

8. And I looked, and behold a pale horse: and his name that sat on him was Death, and Hell followed with him. And power was given unto them over the fourth part of the earth to kill with sword, and with hunger, and with death, and with the beasts of the earth.

This is the natural thing to follow after total evil is released on the earth. Do remember to keep the balances in mind when we get to the mark of the beast. These verses describe what follows the empowering of the slain Antichrist by Satan. Basically, anything goes to enlarge his kingdom on earth or below the surface. One might ask whether these two, Death and Hell, are demons. That's very likely. Remember, this is during the great tribulation, the last half of the tribulation period, and in the evil world, anything goes.

9. And when he had opened the fifth seal, I saw under the altar the souls of them that were slain for the word of God, and for the testimony which they held:
10. And they cried with a loud voice, saying, How long, 0 Lord, holy and true, dost thou not judge and avenge our blood on them that dwell on the earth?
11. And white robes were given unto every one of them; and it was said unto them, that they should rest yet for a little season, until their fellow servants also and their brethren, that should be killed as they were, should be fulfilled.

God is seen in the fifth seal in one of His most important roles. He never forgets or overlooks, and always gives just rewards. Remember in the Jewish sacrifices in Leviticus 4:17, the blood was poured out at the base of the altar.

Dear ones, please grasp the reality that God did not choose for sin to be in His creation. Man made the choice, and God and His creation have suffered. These individuals of verses 9–11 suffered because of the evil of mankind while they served God. As these verses show, their number will grow. Please consider that through the centuries, and in the reality of souls, God has suffered watching the agony of His creation. As 1 John 4, says, *"God is love."*

"And white robes were given unto every one of them." God never forgets. He is a personal God. These verses are a picture of chapter 15, but one thing at a time.

> 12. *And I beheld when he had opened the sixth seal, and, lo, there was a great earthquake; and the sun became black as sackcloth of hair, and the moon became as blood;*
> 13. *And the stars of heaven fell unto the earth, even as a fig tree casteth her untimely figs, when she is shaken of a mighty wind.*
> 14. *And the heaven departed as a scroll when it is rolled together; and every mountain and island were moved out of their places.*
> 15. *And the kings of the earth, and the great men, and the rich men, and the chief captains, and the mighty men, and every bondman, and every free man, hid themselves in the dens and in the rocks of the mountains;*
> 16. *And said to the mountains and rocks, Fall on us, and hide us from the face of him that sitteth on the throne, and from the wrath of the Lamb:*
> 17. *For the great day of his wrath is come; and who shall be able to stand?*

The events of these verses are described in chapters 16–18. The kick-off point is the latter part of chapter 11, with the full description given in chapters 16–18. Please keep an eye out for the ark of God.

One more thing to grasp: At the close of this outline in verse 17 is the lack of the ability of these folks to meet with God. Instead, they can only cringe. Their mindset is to only be afraid. Mankind was created on the sixth day. In the sixth seal is seen the ugly nature of man. Instead of turning to God, they only want to be hidden from Him. That should remind us of a certain couple. God does say His Spirit will not always strive with man. Oh, the hopelessness of these people!

I told you God is logical. This is His own outline.

Chapter 7

1. And after these things I saw four angels standing on the four corners of the earth, holding the four winds of the earth, that the wind should not blow on the earth, nor on the sea, nor on any tree.

2. And I saw another angel ascending from the east, having the seal of the living God: and he cried with aloud voice to the four angels, tow hom it was given to hurt the earth and the sea,

3. Saying, Hurt not the earth, neither the sea, nor the trees, till we have sealed the servants of our God in their foreheads.

This is the preparatory work of God's angels and appears to be the occasion of Daniel 12:1, empowered by the Holy Spirit to accomplish the righteous judgment of God on an ungodly mankind. God is in control, and He does what He wants. The important thing is to realize that there are certain things that have to take place first. We will cover them briefly now and in greater detail later.

Please note that the use of the word *wind* is symbolic of the judgment activity of God, and that God's judgment is thorough. *"The four winds,"* in other words, are all points of the compass.

Chapter 8 is where the actual events of tribulation start taking place, so let me set the stage in chapter 7 with a brief enumeration.

1. The church age is finished, and the Lord comes in the clouds to call out the living and unite the departed believers with their glorified bodies. The living believers will be changed into their glorified bodies *"in the twinkling of an eye."*

2. Michael's battle with Satan and his angels has already taken place. More about that later.

3. There will be two believers, witnesses, left on earth. If you are wondering about this, remember what the Lord said about John the Baptist. Could you be one of these witnesses?

4. The judgment seat of Christ takes place, and rewards are given.

5. The throne of righteousness is set, and all related events are accomplished in order for God to proceed on His time schedule.

6. Now chapter 7's sealing takes place. These 144,000 will not die in the tribulation. They are the remnant that God promises in the Old Testament. Notice, please, that the tribe of Dan is not mentioned. You can see in the Book of Judges that was the very tribe that introduced idolatry into the nation of Israel. Of course, God had to keep His word (see Deut. 29:18–20; Judg. 18).

4. And I heard the number of them which were sealed·
and there were sealed an hundred and forty and four
thousand of all the tribes of the children of Israel.

5. Of the tribe of Juda were sealed twelve thousand. Of the
tribe of Reuben were sealed twelve thousand. Of the
tribe of Gad were sealed twelve thousand.

6. Of the tribe of Asher were sealed twelve thousand. Of
the tribe of Nepthalim were sealed twelve thousand. Of
the tribe of Manasses were sealed twelve thousand.

7. Of the tribe of Simeon were sealed twelve thousand. Of
the tribe of Levi were sealed. twelve thousand. Of the
tribe of Issachar were sealed twelve thousand.

8. Of the tribe of Zabulon were sealed twelve thousand. Of
the tribe of Joseph there were sealed twelve thousand.
Of the tribe of Benjamin were sealed twelve thousand.

The tribes had their good points and bad points, as their father, Israel, explained on his death bed in Genesis 49. The sad thing to say about the tribe of Dan is that even though Israel said he would rule his people, he was also a curse. That tribe followed Adam's example:

    a. They took the easy way out.
    b. They made their decision not to accept judgment, but to seek their own path.

The tribe of Dan gave up, instead of doing the following:

a. Trusting God for the victory
b. Following the way that they had been shown by God

They did nor want to grasp the gift that God had given them. Consequently, Israel will not have one of their tribes assured of being in the thousand-year reign of Christ.

You know, it is hard to realize the possibility of victory if you are dwelling in the land of "what do I want to do?" God said it and that should settle it, for He always provides the means to accomplish His will. Instead, the tribe of Dan will have no representative in the 144,000. God knew all things, and to prepare for this, He gave an extra blessing to Joseph.

Dear ones, we are on this side of the calling out (the rapture). Wouldn't it be better to absolutely know we do not have to rake our chances on the other side of the rapture?

These 144,000 will be seen later. Please note here, they are sealed by God. They will not be hurt by the events of the tribulation, because of that seal. Please consider the first chapter of Ephesians.

> 9. *After this I beheld, and, lo, a great multitude, which no man could number, of all nations, and kindreds, and people, and tongues, stood before the throne, and before the Lamb, clothed with white robes, and palms in their hands;*
> 10. *And cried with a loud voice, saying, Salvation to our God which sitteth upon the throne, and unto the Lamb.*

11. *And all the angels stood round about the throne, and about the elders and the four beasts, and fell before the throne on their faces, and worshipped God,*

12. *Saying, Amen: Blessing, and glory, and wisdom, and thanksgiving, and honour, and power, and might, be unto our God for ever and ever. Amen.*

13. *And one of the elders anwered, saying unto me, What are these which are arrayed in white robes? and whence came they?*

14. *And I said unto him, Sir, thou knowest. And he said to me, These are they which came out of great tribulation, and have washed their robes, and made them white in the blood of the Lamb.*

15. *Therefore are they before the throne of God, and serve him day and night in his temple: and he that sitteth on the throne shall dwell among them.*

16. *They shall hunger no more, neither thirst any more; neither shall the sun light on them, nor any heat.*

17. *For the Lamb which is in the midst of the throne shall feed them, and shall lead them unto living fountaim of waters: and God shall wipe away all tears from their eyes.*

Chapter 7 starts by the setting up of the four angels to cause much harm on the earth. There is a moment given to seal the 144,000, and then God, instead of slashing away at deserving mankind, shows us that there will be a vast multitude saved during the tribulation. God is always ready to save if a person will meet God on His terms.

One sometimes wonders if there will be a special group in heaven because of some deed or something-you know, like Abraham or David or Paul. Please remember that crowns have already been given, thrones will be sat upon, etc.

These, like the rest, have white robes. Because of what they will go through during the tribulation, their faith will be proven. They do have a special place before the throne. We will deal with them in the thousand-year reign of chapter 20. Life in the first half of the tribulation will be extremely hard. Life for folks during the latter half of the tribulation is going to be like nothing that has ever been seen. God has expressed this earlier in His Word.

It is so great to be on this side of this horrific time. Also, it is so great that God cares and provides and keeps His promises. Think of it now: He knew all this before He created man.

Now, are you ready?

Chapter 8

1. And when hehad opened the seventh seal there was silence in heaven about the space of half an hour.

The number seven in the Bible means complete; the actual focus is now on the earth. It is very likely that all that has been addressed heretofore is accomplished in this thirty-minute time period. I do not know that to be the case; it very well could be. Since this is the actual start of the tribulation judgments as seen from the earth's point of view, it is most likely the case. Heaven has to be set for the tribulation, as I stated above. Seven, meaning complete, shows us that God has accomplished everything needed to actually start the tribulation judgments. The book is now open, and all is in order and ready to go. The actual day-by-day events of the tribulation can start happening because the book of God's war of judgment now *is* open.

2. And I saw the seven angels which stood before God; and to them were given seven trumpets.

3. And another angel came and stood at the altar, having a golden censer; and there was given unto him much incense, tha the should offer it with the prayers of all saints upon the golden altar which was before the throne.

4. And the smoke of the incense, which came with the prayers of the saints, ascended up before God out of the angel's hand. [You do see the golden altar of the Old Testament, yes.]

5. And the angel took the censer, and filled it with fire of the altar, and cast it into the earth: and there were voices, and thunderings, and lightnings, and an earthquake.

6. And the seven angels which had the seven trumpets prepared themselves to sound.

Now that the first seven of the book have reached the finishing point, we see the next seven. We have gone from sealing apparatuses to instruments of sound, from completing the releasing to the seven things of drawing attention, or heralding, if you will. One must consider them as commands in the process of battle to win the victory, to accomplish the battle as previously planned.

Here is an awesome picture of the opportunity of man to approach as displayed with the tabernacle. The high priest burned incense as a sweet smell before God. He did so in a prayer of humility before God. He also did so when entering the Holy of Holies once a year. The cloud was to hide God's holiness so the priest would not die from the glory. God could have continued presenting Himself, as He did with Moses. However, He had set up the tabernacle, and this was part of His service. Here we see the angel has our prayers and offers them.

Okay, just how important is prayer? Prayer in humility before God, and seeking His will and pleasure, is represented here. Moses was straightforward with God in his discourse with God after the golden calf incident. Jesus displayed how prayer is to be and in the garden prayed such a prayer. Paul in Romans 8 describes our prayers. Awesome!

Since God knows what we do and the thoughts and intents of our hearts, we should never diminish the importance of honest, simple prayers. God, after answering them one way or another, bottles them up and saves them for later use. Do you see just how precious you are to God?

In the Holy of Holies, there was a rustinct time of covering and judgment, or the rolling forward of judgment. At this moment in heaven, there is only the initiating of judgment. The smoke of the incense pictures the righteousness of God in what is about to happen. Mankind could not look into heaven, of course, but as with the mercy sear, ungodly man cannot see a holy God, for they are not one.

As for the voices, thunderings, lightnings, and an earthquake, if God can't get your attention one way, He will try another. In chapter 4, lightnings, thunders, and voices are explained. God, here in chapter 8, adds an earthquake. Also, if He hasn't gotten your attention on this side of chapter 4, He will in chapter 8. About now, I should interject, it is much too late for oops!

> 7. *The first angel sounded, and there followed hail and fire mingled with blood, and they were cast upon the earth: and the third part of trees was burnt up, and all green grass was burnt up.*

Here, with the old way of looking at the Book of Revelation, there would not have been much left to destroy. I just thought I would throw that in.

God, as you can see, immediately gets mankind's attention. Remember, too, that man is trying to restore order and to have a line of authority. The removal of millions of people is not an easy thing to recover from. The Antichrist of Revelation 6:2 is on the scene and ready to fulfill his destiny. Boy, what a job he is taking on. There are three and a half years between Revelation 6:2 and 6:3.

Then God lays waste to one-third of the trees and all green grass. God hates groves of trees used to assemble for religious services. Now, are they doing that here? I don't know, but it sure was popular in the Old Testament and is still used today. Next is the grass. It sure is hard to grow animals if there is no grass for them to eat, so now we have a major interruption in the food supply. Think of it—these are major occurrences for the world to recover from.

How will the leaders explain this? Furthermore, what will be the thoughts about the hail, the fire, and the blood of verse 7 that these folks can't get away from? Remember, during this time there will be the witnesses mentioned above, who will be fulfilling their job. God always has a witness; are we doing our job today?

8. And the second angel sounded, and as it were a great mountain burning with fire was cast into the sea: and the third part of the sea became blood;

9. And the third part of the creatures which were in the sea, and had Life, died; and the third part of the ships were destroyed.

Do you notice the use of one-third and the effects that are realized on earth? It kind of makes one think of one of the members of the Godhead, doesn't it?

First come hailstones, fire, and blood: one of earth (hail), then fire (a force on earth), and then blood (an important part of actual living).

Now God moves on to bigger things and uses even bigger things to accomplish the job. But the result is the same, devastation by one-third. Killing the sea life is bad enough, but for mankind, the destruction of a mechanism of making money is totally unacceptable.

We will later see man's anguish as to this kind of devastation. People will put up with a lot, as long as it does not happen to themselves personally, but don't touch their money. These events, and the responses to them, do not focus on individuals' needs, but rather on mankind as a whole. God is dealing with mankind as a whole; however, individuals are suffering.

Can one see the actual cold, heartless endeavor of Satan? God became an earthly individual in the flesh in order to be a personal Savior. Satan strove to *enslave* all and did so by one lie (actually more, but he started with one). In the garden, Jesus was selfless; in the tribulation, He is the judge. In the garden of Eden, Satan was selfish and used self-oriented intentions; in the tribulation and at the end of the age, evil is judged. We must move on.

10. And the third angel sounded, and there fell great star from heaven, burning as it were a lamp, and it fell upon the third part of the rivers, and upon the fountains of waters;

*11. And the name of the star is called Wormwood: and the
third part of the waters became wormwood; and many
men died of the waters, because they were made bitter.*

Can you imagine the jubilation of the angels? They once had
to stand by at the cross, but now they are empowered to act. First,
God touches man's pleasant things in life and his production of
food. Next, He goes for his profits. Now, God is touching his
very ability to live. We must have water; now, I wonder why God
would make us so reliant on water? And look at brilliant man:
some died trying to drink the water anyway. Ain't we cards?

*12. And the fourth angel sounded, and the third part of the
sun was smitten, and the thirdpart of the moon, and the
third part of the stars; so as the third part of them was
darkened, and the day shone not for a third part of it,
and the night likewise.*

I wonder, if there is no light, that means what? Well, remember
they killed the Light of the World, so they get darkness for a third
of the day. Remember in chapter 6 about the sun and moon and the
stars; God just won't quit, will He? These will be affected again
later, but God is moving on to the light of man. Man has always
used the sun and moon and the stars as important mechanisms in
his life and worship. Now they will not have these, and again, by
one-third. Man valued the sun, and not the Son. Here again, man
will adapt.

*13. And I beheld, and heard an angel flying through the
midst of heaven, saying with a loud voice, Woe, woe, woe,
to the inhabiters of the earth by reason of the other voices
of the trumpet of the three angels, which are yet to sound!*

Verse 13 heralds three woes that mankind is yet to see. Stop
and think of what man is enduring, and then there comes a
being flying across the sky and pronouncing more devastation

to come. Wow! I'm currently writing a little book about the last ten years of our lives, and I can understand a little of what they are going to be thinking. What next? Well ...

Chapter 9

1. And the fifth angel sounded, and I saw a star fall from heaven unto the earth: and to him was given the key of the bottomless pit.

Remember that chapter 6 mentioned the stars falling, and we have already seen those occurrences. Boy, this one really starts something. Man has endured basically three years of tumultuous devastation just to get to this part. Boy, does it get worse!

Now, some would think that this is Lucifer himself Wouldn't you? Well, it's not. We will cover that later in chapter 17. I think it is a holy angel on God's mission, and why not? Remember, it is God who is in control and handing out judgment.

For the folks who will see this in person and for the billions who realize its occurrence by television broadcasts, what a horror will come over them. They might try to think it could be aliens, but the witnesses will be pointing out where it is coming from.

2. And he opened the bottomless pit; and there arose a smoke out of the pit, as the smoke of a great furnace; and the sun and the air were darkened by reason of the smoke of the pit.

3. And there came out of the smoke Locusts upon the earth: and unto them was given power, as the scorpions of the earth have power.

4. And it was commanded them that they should not hurt the grass of the earth, neither any green thing, neither any tree; but only those men which have not the seal of God in their foreheads.

5. *And to them it was given that they should not kill them, but that they should be tormented five months: and their torment was as the torment of a scorpion, when he striketh a man.*

6. *And in those days shall men seek death, and shall not find it; and shall desire to die, and death shall flee from them.*

7. *And the shapes of the locusts were like unto horses prepared unto battle; and on their heads were as it were crowns like gold, and their faces were as the faces of men.*

8. *And they had hair as the hair of women, and their teeth were as the teeth of lions.*

9. *And they had breastplates, as it were breastplates of iron; and the sound of their wings was as the sound of chariots of many horses running to battle.*

10. *And they had tails like unto scorpions, and there were stings in their tails: and their power was to hurt men five months.*

You know, up to this point, man had God to deal with, and that was bad enough. Now they have critters walking around to look at and be harmed by. As is written, these critters that have never been seen before will wreak havoc for five months. They don't have to eat, these demons, so for them, it's *party time.* Can you imagine the smell of all those demons coming out of that hole? Can you imagine the smell of their approach? Can you imagine the ferocity of their attack? Can you imagine the scene they will leave behind-the pain, the anguish, and the devastation in people's lives? It's not going to be "I just want to touch you with my tail." Yep, it sure is good not to be going through that, but there is more to come.

The 144,000 will not be hurt by these fearsome creatures, but the rest of mankind will suffer big time and will have no escape—no, not even death.

When you think of verses 7–10 and the size of these things—their gruesome look, invulnerability, speed, and sound—think also of their relentless attack and the pain that follows. Do you think that God used the head of a man with the teeth of a lion and the beauty of a woman's hair to send home a point? Man is supposed to be the head over God's creation. The lion, being the king of the beasts, is ready to devour; and a woman's hair is the crown of her beauty, and also equally deceptive.

You've heard of leading and ruling by intimidation. Well, let's see who the leader is.

> *11. And they had a king over them, which is the angel of the bottomless pit, whose name in the Hebrew tongue is Abaddon, but in the Greek tongue hath his name Apollyon.*
> *12. One woe is past; and, behold, there come two woes more hereafter.*

You know evil mankind should be thinking, "Man, this is a bad world we live in." One would think that they would be encouraged to turn to God and away from self and evil. By the way, who do you think this leader is? We'll see.

> *13. And the sixth angel sounded, and I heard a voice from the four horns of the golden altar which is before God,*
> *14. Saying to the sixth angel which had the trumpet, Loose the four angels which are bound in the great river Euphrates.*
> *15. And the four angels were loosed, which were prepared for an hour, and a day, and a month, and a year, for to slay the third part of men.*
> *16. And the number of the army of the horsemen were two hundred thousand strikes: and I heard the number of them.*
> *17. And thus I saw the horses in the vision, and them that sat on them, having breastplates of fire, and of jacinth, and brimstone: and the heads of the horses were as the heads of lions; and out of their mouths issued fire and smoke and brimstone.*
> *18. By these three was the third part of men killed, by the fire, and by the smoke, and by the brimstone, which issued out of their mouths.*
> *19. For their power is in their mouth, and in their tails: for their tails were like unto serpents, and had heads, and with them they do hurt.*

Theses verses are not to be confused with Revelation 16: 12; they are separate situations.

Well, it got a lot worse, didn't it? The river Euphrates must have been crowded. These aresome of Satan's forces, being bound and held for an evil job. They, too, cannot touch the 144,000. Will they kill mainly in the Middle East area, or will they scatter across the globe? Remember, mankind is shrinking and mankind is gathering from across the globe. The usable parts of the globe are shrinking.

These beasts have riders. Is it possible that both rider and horse will have breastplates of brilliant orange fire and brimstone? It is very likely. Will both rider and beast have the power to kill? It is hard to say. However, they have one hour to kill, and they are going to be very vicious. After all, they have been cooped up in the river just waiting since the creation of the world. By rough calculations, they will be killing in the neighborhood of fiveto ten people each; it could be more. Did you notice that they have only an hour to accomplish this because the first half of the tribulation is closing? Their number will be two hundred million.

Their work has to be accomplished quickly because a different way of life is coming on the scene.

> *20. And the rest of the men which were not killed by these plagues yet repented not of the works of their hands, that they should not worship devils, and idols of gold, and silver, and brass, and stone, and of wood: which neither can see, nor hear, nor walk:*
>
> *21. Neither repented they of their murders, nor of their sorceries, nor of their fornication, nor of their thefts.*

While being attacked, those who survive will still refrain from repenting, as we see in verse 21. Isn't mankind cute? Not! This is at the end of the first three and half years of tribulation. Mankind is still thinking they are in or can gain control. Or is it that they, just like us today, a.re too stubborn to surrender to God being a reality? What would those people say to us today if they could?

But look also, with all the death and horrors happening, their mindset is still to kill, to use witchcraft and Satanism to harm others, to party hearty, and to steal. Yep, mankind just never learns.

Let's take a quick analysis of this period of life on earth:

1. God has been killing and destroying.
2. Satan and his forces have been killing and harming.
3. Mankind has been killing and accomplishing great harm on each other, as is seen in these last two verses. They will be looking for a place to hide, but can't.

One asks why one does one not want to come to grips with God in the age in which we live. "We've got it made," or "I'll deal with God when I see Him" is a common response. But you might think of this: no one knows when He is going to take out His believers and the tribulation will start. It could be *today*. You should be able to see by now, in these folk's lives, that everyone is the *enemy*. My friend, if you do not know Christ as your Savior, why not now? Please!

Chapter 10

This is an exciting chapter. The Lord Jesus Himself is seen in a way that is rich with seriousness. I believe the Lord Jesus in the Book of Revelation is claiming His creation back from the kingdoms that have ruled over it from Nimrod to the present.

1. *I. And I saw another mighty angel come down from heaven, clothed with a cloud: and a rainbow was upon his head, and his face was as it were the sun, and his feet as pillars of fire:*
2. *And he had in his hand a Little book open: and he set his right foot upon the sea, and his Left foot on the earth,*
3. *And cried with a Loud voice, as when a Lion roareth: and when he had cried, seven thunders uttered their voices.*
4. *And when the seven thunders had uttered their voices, I was about to write: and I heard a voice from heaven saying unto me, Seal up those things which the seven thunders uttered, and write them not.*
5. *And the angel which I saw stand upon the sea and upon the earth Lifted up his hand to heaven,*
6. *And sware by him that liveth far ever and ever, who created heaven, and the things that therein are, and the earth, and the things that therein are, and the sea, and the things which are therein, that there should be time no longer:*
7. *But in the days of the voice of the seventh angel, when he shall begin to sound, the mystery of God should be finished, as he hath declared to his servants the prophets.*

Is this the Lord? Yes, of course. The Creator, the Lord of Israel, has to now start Jacob's trouble. The supplanter is now being judged. They turned from idols, and instead of seeing their Messiah, they saw self and gain. The little book is the proclamation of the start of Jacob's trouble. Dear ones, as we see the failures and frailty of Israel, we see ourselves.

Why is He clothed with a cloud? The Lord Jesus Christ, on many occasions, used the cloud in dealing directly with humans, and will do so again. When talking with Moses, the Lord used a cloud to keep His glory from killing Moses.

The tabernacle had the cloud of smoke. The Lord had already used the cloud when He brought the children of Israel out of Egypt. In chapter 8, when the angel offered the prayers, the incense caused a cloud that ascended before God. As great as mankind is, we cannot stand before the holy God. God's love is revealed in His having gone through the judgment of the cross, hence the rainbow and feet as pillars of fire, also seen as fine brass in chapter 1.

The scene is the same as the one of the Lord in chapter 1. However, what you would think represents the deity of the Lord is covered; the golden girdle is covered. Where should our focus be centered then? The rainbow represents the beauty and the splendor, the totality of light (which is life and power) of the Lord Jesus, His beautiful head and face that had been so marred and thorn pierced. My dear ones, if that doesn't cause tears to flow, what will?

Our focus is to be on the following:

1. The face of the sun is the power of the Lord Jesus—all power.
2. The feet are pillars of fire, as the righteous judge, the one that none can stand before and challenge for the right to be judge or to judge.

The important thing to see is chat the Lord is claiming ownership and authority, and is expressing His power for all to see. I do not chink it is parenthetical or a picture of a future scene.

The Lord has allowed and has brought mankind to this point and now steps forward co begin the last part of the judgment of mankind. Remember, this is right on the verge of the midway point of the tribulation. Why, you ask, is God doing this at this point in time? Hasn't mankind already gone through such an ordeal? Oh yes; however, sin was not by God's choice and must bedealt with. Looking at Daniel 12:6, look where the individual is standing. He is standing on the waters in the river (the river represents all of mankind). Now look where the Lord is standing: the right foot on the sea and the left foot on the land, God of all creation.

Now consider Matthew 24:4–21, in particular verses 15–21:

15. When ye therefore shaft see the abomination of desolation, spoken of by Daniel the prophet, stand in the holy place, (whoso readeth, let him understand:)

16. Then let them which be in Judea flee into the mountains:

17. Let him which is on the housetop not come down to take anything out of his house:

18. Neither let him which is in the field return back to take his clothes.

19. And woe unto them that are with child, and to them that give suck in those days!

20. But pray ye that your flight be not in the winter, neither on the sabbath day:

21. For then shaft be great tribulation, such as was not since the beginning of the world to this time, no, nor ever shall be.

Picture this with me, please. Not the Lamb, but the Lord of glory is standing on the sea and the land, holrung the opened prophesied book of the end of sin (Daniel's sealed book). The voice from heaven says not to write what the thunders have revealed, but the Lord says that there shall be rime no longer. Just as the Lord said, *"It is finished"* in John 19:30, having finished all the sufferings mentioned in the Old Testament, He now is proclaiming the midway point of the tribulation, hence Jacob's trouble. You see, He has the authority to say, *"It is finished"* and to initiate Jacob's trouble. And praise God He will say, "It is done."

> 8. *And the voice which I heard from heaven spake unto me again, and said, Go and take the little book which is open in the hand of the angel which standeth upon the sea and upon the earth.*
> 9. *And I went unto the angel and said unto him, Give me the little book. And he said unto me, Take it, and eat it up; and it shall make thy belly bitter, but it shall be in thy mouth sweet as honey.*
> 10. *And I took the little book out of the angel's hand, and ate it up; and it was in my mouth sweet as honey: and as soon as I had eaten it, my belly was bitter.*
> 11. *And he said unto me, Thou must prophesy again before many peoples, and nations, and tongues, and kings.*

Two questions come to mind with these verses: why will the book have these effects on John, and how is it that John will testify again? The first is that God is finishing His work and word; there will be victory for God's creation. The second is that it is said that John was boiled in oil—evidently, after his experience on Patmos, so he had to have gone back to the mainland. It was great that God would finish His word and work; it was sad what was about to happen to John's nation, as stated in Luke 13:34–35:

> 34. *O Jerusalem, Jerusalem which killest the prophets, and stonest them that are sent unto thee; how often would I have gathered thy children together, a sa hen doth gather her brood under wings, and ye would not!*
> 35. *Behold your house is left unto you desolate: and verily I say unto you, Ye shall not see me, until the time come when ye shall say, Blessed is he that cometh in the name of the Lord.*

Chapter 11

As we begin the eleventh chapter, we must use Jeremiah 6:7–16 and Matthew 27:25. What a sad occasion. Please consider also Luke 19:12–27. I'll let you look that up.

First is Jeremiah 6:7–16:

7. As a fountain casteth out her waters, so she casteth out her wickedness: violence and spoil is heard in her; before me continually is grief and wounds.

8. Be thou instructed, 0 Jerusalem, lest my soul depart from thee; lest I make thee desolate, a land not inhabited.

9. This saith the LORD of hosts, They shall thoroughly glean the remnant of Israel as a vine: turn back thine hand as a grape gatherer into the baskets.

10. To whom shall I speak, and give warning, that they may hear? Behold, their ear is uncircumcised, the word of the LORD is unto them a reproach; they have no delight in it.

11. Therefore am I full of the fury of the LORD; I am weary with holding in: I will pour it out upon the children abroad, and upon the assembly of young men together: for even the husband with the wife shall be taken, the aged with him that is full of days.

12. And their houses shall be turned unto others, with their fields and wives together: for I will stretch out my hand upon the inhabitants of the land, saith the LORD.

13. For from the least of them even unto the greatest of them every one is given to covetousness;

14. They have healed also the hurt of the daughter of my people slightly, saying, Peace, peace; when there is no peace.

15. Were they ashamed when they had committed abomination? nay they were not at all ashamed, neither could they blush: therefore they shall fall among them tl1at fall: at the time that I visit them they shall be cast down, saith the LORD.

16. Thus saith the LORD, Stand ye in the ways, and see, and ask for the old paths, where is the good way, and walk therein, and ye shall find rest for your souls. But they said, We will not walk therein.

Then, Matthew 27:25 says, *"Then answered all the people, and said, His blood be on us, and on our children."*

My, hasn't chat been the case? Now, does chat cell you the extent chat the Lamb of God will go to in order to bring to justice those who reject Him? This is His beloved city, the mountain of peace. God loved mankind so much He lay down and stretched forth His arms on a cross and became a bridge for us all. Someone say amen!

1. *And there was given me a reed like unto a rod: and the angel stood, saying, Rise, and measure the temple of God, and the altar, and them that worship therein.*

2. *But the court which is without the temple leave out, and measure it not; for it is given unto the Gentiles: and the holy city shall they tread under foot forty and two months.*

This is a scene that is at the very end of me first half of me tribulation. The Book of Daniel shows that the Antichrist, in order to have peace, will *allow* them their sacrifice, and to be a nation. They will not be allowed to have their city, Jerusalem, as these two verses show. They will have a structured peace and their city, but the Gentile power will have a controlling factor, measured by a reed. It will include the temple and the altar and the people serving. They will claim peace, but it will be a false peace, again fulfilling Old Testament Scripture.

3. *And I will give power unto my two witnesses, and they shall prophesy a thousand two hundred and threescore days, clothed in sackcloth.*

4. *These are the two olive trees, and the two candlesticks standing before the God of the earth.*

5. *And if any man will hurt them, fire proceedeth out of their mouth, and devoureth their enemies: and if any man will hurt them, he must in this manner be killed.*

As John the Baptist was an actual man, he was born, as will these two be. John the Baptist died. Granted, Elijah did have to come back, as is told in Malachi, the fourth chapter. Does God send His Spirit back into John? Remember what the Lord explained in Matthew, the eleventh chapter. However, Elijah was not commissioned to come back twice. He and Enoch were the only ones allowed to leave this life without death, and that pictures the rapture of the church age believers.

The witnesses will be God's method of dispensing grace, remembering the candlesticks of chapter 1 and Zechariah 4. I do not believe in a partial rapture; two out of millions does not make a partial. These are specially sanctioned believers, who, like all, will have to die. These two are the fulfilling of the last verse of Psalm 22.

These two witnesses have been standing for righteousness for three and a half years, the first half of the tribulation period. They are protected by God with the power that God gave them. Will their power be that actual fire will come out of their mouths, or will they just have to speak and their attackers die? Like the Lord in chapter 1 and the two-edged sword, it will probably be their words empowered by God, and they do their miracles by speaking.

6. *These have power to shut heaven, that it rain not in the days of their prophecy: and have power over waters to turn them to blood, and to smite the earth with all plagues, as often as they will.*

7. And when they shall have finished their testimony, the beast that ascendeth out of the bottomless pit shall make war against them, and shall overcome them, and kill them.

8. And their dead bodies shall lie in the street of the great city, which spiritually is called Sodom and Egypt, where also our Lord was crucified.

9. And they of the people and kindreds and tongues and nations shall see their dead bodies three days and an half, and shall not suffer their dead bodies to be put in graves.

10. And they that dwell upon the earth shall rejoice over them, and make merry, and shall send gifts one to another; because these two prophets tormented them that dwelt on the earth.

11. And after three days and an half the Spirit of life from God entered into them, and they stood upon their feet; and great fear fell upon them which saw them.

12. And they heard a great voice from heaven saying unto them, Come up hither. And they ascended up to heaven in a cloud; and their enemies beheld them.

Their ministry is over, and the king of the beasts that came out of the bottomless pit will end their service in the city of Jerusalem. The Lord, in all of time, has never left the earth without a witness. Their job has been to serve in the mainstream of life, and it is now over. These two will be such pests to ungodly mankind. You notice that they have power to cause drought and different plagues; this refers back to Elijah and Moses.

Satan, as seen in verse 7, will be allowed to kill the two witnesses, and mankind will rejoice. What a rejoicing that these two have stood for righteousness and have proclaimed it steadfastly. Ungodly mankind's rejoicing lasts but a short while; you see, God always gets the last laugh. This will be such a perplexing situation for "conquering" mankind, to see their dead prey stand and rise, and that after three and a half days. The bodies should have been bloated by then. Will man hear the voice? I do not know, but they will still be overwhelmed by the sight they see. God knows how to get the victory.

13. And the same hour was there a great earthquake, and the tenth part of the city fell, and in the earthquake were slain ofmen seven thousand: and the remnant were affrighted, and gave glory to the God of heaven.

14. The second woe is past; and, behold, the third woe cometh quickly.

Isn't it neat? Mankind, after seeing the ascension of the two witnesses, is given the opportunity to get all shook up. Seven thousand die, which means God is satisfied with the impression left upon man. They had joy, they had awe, and then they had to stare death in the face, which forced them, just as it did Pharaoh, to give glory to God. However, as with Pharaoh's occasion, it was a shallow glory.

15. And the seventh angel sounded; and there were great voices in heaven, saying, The kingdoms ofthis world are become the kingdoms of our Lord, and of his Christ; and he shall reign for ever and ever.

16. And the four and twenty elders, which sat before God on their seats, fell upon their faces, and worshipped God,

17. Saying, We give thee thanks, 0 Lord God Almighty, which art, and wast, and art to come; because thou hast taken to thee thy great power, and hast reigned.

18. And the nations were angry, and thy wrath is come, and the time of the dead, that they should be judged, and that thou shouldest give reward un to thy servants the prophets, and to the saints, and them that fear thy name, small and great;and shouldest destroy them which destroy the earth.

19. And the temple of God was opened in heaven, and there was seen in his temple the ark of his testament: and there were lightnings, and voices, and thunderings, and an earthquake, and great hail.

What a sight to behold. Remember in the tenth chapter, I mentioned that the Lord, proclaiming His lordship, would be validated in this chapter. Here it is. From the place of all real power come great voices proclaiming God is taking possession of all. I'm going to start at the bottom and go up.

This is the start of the last half of the tribulation, and it is initiated by *"lightnings, and voices, and thunderings, and an earthquake, and great hail."* (God added another item to the proclamation.) This is power being expressed, but is it a show? No. It is a release of righteousness against evil. You see the ark, the container, the "Bearer-Up." The testimony of God is now able to be seen. The jubilation of heaven shows that the end of evil is now corning forth.

One should ask, why is it that the ark has not been seen before now? We have the mercy seat and the Word of God, the Bible. The testimony represents the Word of God. So why is it such a big deal about the ark being seen? In the mechanism to shroud the presence and glory of God, the ark was the final stop. *This* is the starting place of the end of all of God's efforts to finish the sin-ridden life Adam caused.

Man will worship anything and everything but God. The ark represents God on earth, the mercy seat, the testimony, the power. Man would sooner worship these than the holy God and His ordered worship. The ark could not be touched without death befalling the one touching, except for a certain family in the tribe of Levi. It is very befitting for the ark to come on the scene at this point. Please notice the ark alone is seen, meaning the mercy seat has been taken off, which we have already discussed.

That is why verses 15–18 are proclaiming the glory of God and His righteousness in doing these things to creation. Who would ever have the right to take possession, to actually give harmful rewards (damnation) for unrighteous deeds, other than the One who actually did the creating? Verse 18 should be stressed; *"And the nations were angry, and thy wrath is come, and the time of the dead, that they should be judged, and that thou shouldest give reward unto thy servants the prophets, and to the saints, and them that fear thy name, small and great; and shouldest destroy them which destroy the earth."*

I give you Daniel 7:14: *"And there was given him dominion, and glory, and a kingdom, that all people, nation, and languages, should serve him: his dominion is an everlasting dominion, which shall, not pass away, and his kingdom that which shall not be destroyed."*

Sin causes destruction. Accepting Christ brings rewards.

And finally, "The kingdoms of this world are become the kingdoms of our Lord, and of his Christ; and he shall reign for ever and ever." This part of verse 15 is very befitting for the seventh trumpet and the start of the last half of the tribulation. It shows the taking of power and the exercising thereof.

Let me make a short interjection here. Above, when the verse says, *"and shoudest destroy them which destroy the earth,"* we will see later that mankind will stop at nothing to satisfy its desires.

We have seen several sevens thus far. In the next two chapters, there are seven personages to consider before we can continue. In fact, in chapters 12, 13, and 14, we are shown some important events. These are information chapters. They explain what has taken place at this point in time. They set the stage for God's actions for the last half of the tribulation. It is so neat to finally see the rhythm of the Book of Revelation.

Chapter 12

1. And there appeared a great wonder in heaven; a woman clothed with the sun, and the moon under her feet, and upon her head a crown of twelve stars:

2. And she being with child cried, travailing in birth, and pained to be delivered

Of course, this *first personage* is the nation of Israel. Isn't it strange how a nation's history is summed up in two verses? Nations come and go, and often times with not that much of an influence, on the world around them. The nation of Israel has a history line of some three thousand years, depending on how far you want to go. Yet their existence is brought to point in two verses, and they messed that up. We humans are just human. But, in reality, if they had accepted their Messiah, prophecy would not have been fulfilled. You see, the human experience is steadied on the facts, past or future. We have hope only by seeing what God has done or will do, and being able to see or remember what has been prophesied. Should we be so critical of the Israeli nation? No. There had to be a holy sacrifice to remedy creation. Israel was the vehicle by which God would accomplish His plan. Since their decision was like Eve and Adam's, they have suffered and will suffer, *but* it was their choice. Mankind is so prideful of himself, as is the nation of Israel. What about you and me?

3. And there appeared another wonder in heaven; and behold a great red dragon, having seven heads and ten horns, and seven crowns upon his heads.

4. And his tail drew the third part of the stars of heaven, and did cast them to the earth: and the dragon stood before the woman which was ready to be delivered, for to devour her child as soon as it was born.

We will go into much detail concerning this second personage, the dragon of verse 3, in chapter 17, so please be patient. As far as verse 4 and Lucifer trying to kill the Christ child and trying to get Jesus to serve him, and all the other assaults, one can find those accounts in the Gospels. We are not going to go through all that here. The important thing to see is the personages and time zones.

5. And she brought forth a man child, who was to rule all nations with a rod of iron: and her child was caught up unto God, and to his throne.
6. And the woman fled into the wilderness, where she hath a place prepared of God, that they should feed her there a thousand two hundred and threescore days.

You notice that there is nothing mentioned of the cross and taking captivity captive; here again, so much is capsulized in one verse. The key point to realize is that in God's purpose, the Godhead chose what action would be taken to bring creation to a righteous conclusion. It is called sovereignty.

The *third personage,* the man child, is seen in verse 5. We see in one verse the action taken toward Israel. As a whole, the nation of Israel will have no real power at this time and will barely be able to have their sacrifices. To the nation at that time, that will be a triumph. Look at what they are going through today for peace; their peace is never going to be substantial until they accept the true Messiah, and that won't be until the great battle. They will not do this as a nation until He comes in chapter 19. In this chapter's happening, some do. But because they are so devastated, I'm not sure it can be said that they as a nation will have.

The actions of a few stuck-up, prideful people have cost so much to an entire nation for two thousand years. Please keep in mind they had the prophecies as a nation; the people crusted their leaders, instead of God. Does that sound a little like Adam? However, they made their own choice, and the results have lasted a long time. We should really consider carefully our decisions. Let me interject here a thought. When Jesus was twelve, He tried to stimulate the elders' thinking of Scripture. They still clung to tradition and not Scripture. They considered the temple commerce and not truth.

The *fourth personage* is the 144,000 sealed individuals. They are the representatives of the nation who are in a prepared place. Their heritage will be able to be counted back to the eleven sons of Jacob, with one of those sons (Joseph) being represented by two sons. Dan's position was lost because of his tribe introducing idolatry into the nation.

They will not be touched by violence, and for the first half of the tribulation, they will be accessible, to a certain extent. Their security becomes much more involved in the next three and half years. The mention of 1,260 days is the last half of the tribulation period. The first 1,260 days are important, and the 144,000 will have a job to do in public. However, they will have to be totally secured in the last half. If God wanted to, He could hide a candy bar in front of my nose, and I would never find it.

> 7. *And there was war in heaven: Michael and his angels fought against the dragon; and the dragon fought and his angels,*
>
> 8. *And prevailed not; neither was their place found any more in heaven.*
>
> 9. *And the great dragon was cast out, that old serpent, called the Devil, and Satan, which deceiveth the whole world: he was cast out into the earth, and his angels were cast out with him.*
>
> 10. *And I heard a loud voice saying in heaven, Now is come salvation, and strength, and the kingdom of our God, and the power of his Christ: for the accuser of our brethren is cast down, which accused them before our God day and night.*

> 11. And they overcame him by the blood of the Lamb, and
> by the word of their testimony; and they loved not their
> lives unto the death.
>
> 12. Therefore rejoice, ye heavens, and ye that dwell in them.
> Woe to the inhabiters of the earth and of the sea! for
> the devil is come down unto you, having great wrath,
> because he knoweth that he hath but a short time.

Now hang on. There is so much to cover. Boy, ain't it gettin' good?

I have said that Lucifer has been cast out of the presence of God, and he and his angels have been put in the bottomless pit. Maybe you scoffed a bit. The proof of that is seen here, in the next set of verses, and in chapter 17. Let's look closely.

Michael is the *fifth personage*. There is a battle, and no place will be found for the dragon or his angels in heaven; they are cast into the earth. The heralding of the victory is concerned with those of the age before the tribulation starts. Why do I say that, you ask? You see in verse 10 that the kingdom of our God and the power of His Christ is come to power. This cannot be unless the god of this world has been captured.

Think for a minute. God created this world, and man was put in charge of it. Lucifer did not have power in this creation, only with his angels, and that was against God and His angels. Now tell me who is going to win. God, of course. So, if God is going to end the effect of sin in and on His creation, He is going to have to effect a means of a test. Can you imagine the bliss if man had not sinned? If only Adam had chosen the Tree of Life and not the Tree of the Knowledge of Good and Evil.

God's ways are higher than ours, and He alone knows the future; He alone is perfectly holy. There is a big responsibility that comes with a choice, a will. Adam chose wrongly, as we probably would if we were in his shoes. Therefore, we end up with the following fact in 1 Peter 5:8: *"because your adversary the devil, as a roaring lion, walketh about, seeking whom he may devour"* simply because the headship of this world was relinquished to Lucifer by Adam acting on his desire instead of believing God and following Him. Eve's purpose and Adam's decision are seen in the driving force of Nimrod and all the rest.

Looking for the validity of the position and power of Lucifer in and on the world? Please remember the experience of Job and the temptation of our Lord.

I must put here the time that Satan was cast out of heaven. Surely you were wondering when Satan was not allowed to see God in person hence when he was not allowed in heaven. John 12:31 says, *"Now is the judgment of this world: now shall the prince of this world be cast out."* In the tabernacle and the temple, only one person was allowed in the Holy of Holies when the blood was offered, as stated in Leviticus 4:6. Sin has been paid. It remains paid; that is why we are in the throne of grace period. But we have an enemy, as we've already seen 1 Peter 5:8. Satan had no choice about being confined to creation and out of heaven. Remember, leaven could not be found in the Jewish houses during the Passover. The veil is opened, and as we see in Hebrews 4, it says, "Let us come boldly." Are our sins seen? Yes, but they are under the blood (Rom. 5:9). Satan also knows his time is short. We must go on.

We must conclude chat Satan is put somewhere. Only when Satan is defeated and cast our can heaven rejoice, which we see in verse 12. Heaven can rejoice, but woe to the earth. Chapter 13 will give us more on Lucifer's actions on earth, and chapter 17 will finalize these thoughts.

Let us look at the presence of Lucifer (Satan, the devil):

a. After his fall by trying to take God's throne, he was not allowed in God's presence, at the throne of God.

b. When God created mankind, and himself being a created being, Lucifer could approach these newly created beings that had been given authority over this. As we know, he got these beings to follow his will.

c. Mankind having sinned, giving authority over their world to Lucifer, made it a necessity that Lucifer not only be present in this world, but before the judge of this world. We see that in the Book of Job.

89

d. As we saw in the above passage in John, when the sacrificial Lamb of God was preparing to bring the blood into the heavenly Holy of Holies, Lucifer was no longer allowed in heaven. The access of mankind to the Holy of Holies is verified by the tearing of the veil of the temple. It being torn by God is shown in that it was torn from the top to the bottom.

e. Lucifer's presence not being allowed during the first three years and five months of the tribulation period has been seen in chapter 9.

In verses 13–16, we can see the treatment of the Jews for the last two thousand years, as well as what his intensity will be like in the great tribulation. Certainly, Israel has suffered, as has all of mankind. The evil mindset of "I will live my way" is refreshed by the urgency of these last days. Satan has to make God fail; he has to destroy Israel.

> *13. And when the dragon saw that he was cast unto the earth, he persecuted the woman which brought forth the man child.*
>
> *14. And to the woman were given two wings of a great eagle, that she might fly into the wilderness, into her place, where she is nourished for a time, and times, and half a time, from the face of the serpent.*
>
> *15. And the serpent cast out of his mouth water as a flood after the woman, that he might cause her to be carried away of the flood*
>
> *16. And the earth helped the woman, and the earth opened her mouth, and swallowed up the flood which the dragon cast out of his mouth.*

Here, I believe, is the basic account of the second-half activities of Lucifer trying to destroy Israel as a whole, but certainly, believing Israel. This is the 144,000 and possibly some of their converts. What they leave behind in the nation of Israel will be a core of believers and nonbelievers who will face the most horrendous persecution yet.

The 144,000 will be hidden away from the face of the dragon. Up until that time, they were in sight. That was with Lucifer in the bottomless pit and theAntichrist trying to win the support of the world. He will hold things together. He is given power, and he conquers by persuasion and force, all the while God is executing judgment on the world and definitely affecting his kingdom.

Verses 15 and 16 mention a flood. I believe that in the first half of the tribulation, Saran will cast a great army against the sealed of Israel, and God will use the earth to swallow the army. It is neat to be playing on the winning ream, and especially for these folks. God has hidden Israel in the world, as was done in Egypt. Will they have hard times? Yes, I think so. God always provides for Hi sown: *"where she is nourished for a time, and times, and half a time,,from the face of the serpent."* God is good, Satan is evil, hard times are coming. Are you ready?

> *17. And the dragon was wroth with the woman, and went to make war with the remnant of her seed, which keep the commandments of God, and have the testimony of Jesus Christ.*

Unable to harm the woman, the dragon will have to attack the remnant back in the land of Israel. What a difficult life these folks will have. However, they have three things that are said about them:

1. They are a remnant, or a small part.
2. They do have a will, or dedication—the commandments, the Word of God.
3. They have a possession—the testimony of Jesus Christ.

In this one short verse is summed up such tragedy, such suffering. In Daniel 11:31–35, you can see the extent of harm to believers exacted by evil mankind:

31. *And arms shall stand on his part, and they shall pollute the sanctuary of strength, and shall take away the daily sacrifice, and they shall place the abomination that maketh desolate.*
32. *And such as do wickedly against the covenant shall he corrupt by flatteries: but the people that do know their God shall be strong, and do exploits.*
33. *And they that understand among the people shall instruct many: yet they shall fall by the sword, and by flame, by captivity, and by spoil, many days.*
34. *Now when they shall fall they shall be holpen with a little help: but many shall cleave to them with flatteries.*
35. *And some of them of understanding shall fall, to try them, and to purge, and to make them white, even to the time of the end: because it is yet for a time appointed.*

Every effort possible will be used to destroy the little country called Israel. Isn't it strange? The very powerful Satan-indwelled Antichrist will not be able to get the job done. Remember, folks, it's going to be God's way or the very broad way to damnation. God always gets the job done. You reckon that's because He's *God*.

Chapter 13

1. And I stood upon the sand of the sea, and saw a beast rise up out of the sea, having seven heads and ten horns, and upon his horns ten crowns, and upon his heads the name of blasphemy

2. And the beast which I saw was like unto a leopard, and his feet were as the feet of a bear, and his mouth as the mouth of a lion: and the dragon gave him his power, and his seat, and great authority.

The *sixth personage* is now seen. Boy, would I like to get into explaining the seven-headed beast, but all in due time. Of course, the sea is mankind, and not the actual water; the Beast is a regular human being (Dan. 7:3). This Beast represents both the Middle Eastern nations and the European nations, of course. When the Antichrist gains control and becomes the central figure, then it's a one-man show.

What were the main traits mentioned in Daniel?

1. Nebuchadnezzar—total uniqueness (maybe royalty); the mouth of a lion, hence authoritative.
2. Persian—feet of a bear; steady, sure, massive power
3. Greece—sleek, swift, and agile; can handle anything.
4. Roman—efficient, brutal, purposeful. The end-time Roman Empire (feet of clay and iron) will be in a weakened condition until the Antichrist comes forward.

One would ask about the oil-rich Arabian countries. They have their own coalition; however, the real money will be able to control product flow to the extent that the oil coalition will follow. These leaders will set up an individual who later will turn as a Hitler.

It says in verse 2 that "the dragon gave him his power, and his seat, and great authority." The Antichrist has a demon, remember, and it is going to be persuasive. We saw in 6:2 that he already had a bow (military position) and that he was given a crown (an exalted position). Boy, does that reek of Hitler. According to Daniel, he will succeed by persuasion; he will excel. He will get the world going again in the first three and a half years, and then he will start thinking majestic thoughts.

> *3. And I saw one of his heads as it were wounded to death; and his deadly wound was healed: and all the world wondered after the beast.*
>
> *4. And they worshipped the dragon which gave power unto the beast: and they worshipped the beast, saying, Who is like unto the beast? who is able to make war with him?*
>
> *5. And there was given unto him a mouth speaking great things and blasphemies; and power was given unto him to continue forty and two months.*
>
> *6. And he opened his mouth in blasphemy against God, to blaspheme his name, and his tabernacle, and them that dwell in heaven.*
>
> *7. And it was given unto him to make war with the saints, and to overcome them: and power was given him over all kindreds, and tongues, and nations.*

The Beast, the Antichrist, the one who was given a crown in chapter 6, is going to be killed by a sword. Who initiates the assassination is nor as important as the outcome. Lucifer will enter the now dead Antichrist and make him alive, with one exception: the Beast now has tremendous power. The important thing to see is the adoration of the people of the Beast that *cannot* die: *"who is able to make war with hirn?"* The nations that put him in power will be at his call now.

Finally, the devil has the adoration and worship that he has wanted all along. Openly, fervently, Lucifer will be worshiped as their god, except for one thing: he is in a human body and not in his actual estate. Foiled again–that boy just can't win for losing.

This human body, kept alive by the indwelling of Lucifer, is going to speak openly against the God of the two witnesses. God allows him *"forty and two months."* Verse 6 says that he bad mouths those who dwell in heaven, which means he does not have access to heaven.

Just as the rest of the Godhead had to allow Christ to hang on that cross, the Godhead allows things to happen in life. All things, you ask? Yes, because the Godhead is in control of all things. That is why verse 7 says, *"And it was given unto him to make war with the saints."* This is expressed in Daniel 11:30–35. If God is in control, then why do bad things happen to His people? Do remember that we are the ones who choose to do wrong.

Study the above-mentioned verses. In all of life, God has a purpose. Sometimes we have hard times that just don't make sense, and sometimes it is for our correction. It is always for a purpose and for our growth. The Lord Jesus in the Gospels expresses God's attitude for our lives when He asks whether a father would give his child a stone for a piece of bread. The time that we are studying will be such a hard time; however, there is One who is in control.

One major point to focus on is that battered mankind will finally have a leader who stands proudly and boldly, and is unkillable. Their thoughts, as expressed in verses 4 and 5, are a result of their not wanting to answer to the true and living God in the first place. So what if there is a little blasphemy? Think for a moment about those who flippantly say, "What about Jesus?" Oh, please remember, *God does not forget or overlook anything.*_

8. And all that dwell upon the earth shall worship him, whose names are not written in the book of life of the Lamb slain from the foundation of the world.

9. If any man have an ear, let him hear.

10. He that leadeth into captivity shall go into captivity: he that killeth with the sword must be killed with the sword. Here is the patience and the faith of the saints.

It is so good to belong on God's good side and to have your name in His book. But look at the opposite: those who are not written in His book will worship the Beast. Big mistake, but they have made their choice and will receive the results that must come from their action–all with an end in destruction. Folks, we sure need to win others.

The key thought of verse 9 is this: do you and I have a heart for searching for truth?

Verse 10 shows an inlportant point to focus on; chat is, *"if the Son shall set you free, you shall be free indeed"* (John 8:36). God will see that the leader into captivity will meet with captivity. Furthermore, those who willfully take lives will meet with the same "couldn't care less" attitude.

This verse must be something of a "reaping what a person sows" message. But there is something we must see: this verse is a private message to the godly of this time. It is also a verse of encouragement to the godly: there is one who is in control, so *hang on. Look up. Speak out.*

11. And I beheld another beast coming up out of the earth; and he had two horns like a lamb, and he spake as a dragon.

The *seventh personage* is the lesser beast. Not coming out of the sea means it is not a world leader or king, but instead a person of a notable position. Notice it has two horns, meaning it has power or holds a position of authority. The speaking as a dragon links it with the first dragon and the demeanor of the dragon. It will not be a good person, but it will be a powerful person. He will have a religious position. His desire and purpose is to worship the Beast, which equals the Antichrist.

12. *And he exerciseth allt he power of the first beast before him, and causeth the earth and them which dwell therein to worship the first beast, whose deadly wound was healed*

13. *And he doeth great wonders, so that he maketh fire come down from heaven on the earth in the sight of men,*

14. *And deceiveth them that dwell on the earth by the means of those miracles which he had power to do in the sight of the beast; saying to them that dwell on the earth, that they should make an image to the beast, which had the wound by a sword, and did live.*

15. *And he had power to give life unto the image of the beast, that the image of the beast should both speak, and cause that as many as would not worship the image of the beast should be killed*

16. *And he causeth all, both small and great, rich and poor, free and bond, to receive a mark in their right hand, or in their foreheads:*

17. *And that no man might buy or sell, save he that had the mark, or the name of the beast, or the number of his name.*

18. *Here is wisdom. Let him that hath understanding count the number of the beast: for it is the number of a man; and his number is Six hundred threescore and six.*

In the Bible, the number six represents mankind and the beasts of the earth. Think of the number 666 as the Godhead saying, "You are just a man." He is going to be walking around thinking he is something, and all the while God will be laughing. While it is so that a person is represented here, it does give a focal point for evil mankind to grasp.

As far as the tribulation period is concerned, the second half is just getting started, and the evil side is the first one to get moving. This new beast, the seventh personage, just happens to be the False Prophet.

His job is to enhance the first beast. Satan, the one indwelling the Antichrist, has the initiative to do everything that is needed to be done. Then why is the second beast needed? With any adoration situation, it always is best to have another person to stand with you and for you to act as a buffer, and also, to get the adoration going. lhat is what this beast's purpose is going to be. Is this a religious person? More than likely it is. We are told he *"causeth the earth and them which dwell therein to worship the first beast."* Is it a leader out of the Roman Catholic Church? He probably is.

Mankind has a built-in drive to worship, even if it is self. It is usually something that can be looked up to orfeared. Another point is that since Adam's sin, there has always been an evil religious *institution.* This individual is going to be the head of it. This person, this beast, will be the initiator of whatever the Beast wants.

The headquarters of theAntichrist will be in the old Babylon area according to Zechariah 5:5ff. Is this going to be the place of the great whore? I think so. Rome would be a more accessible place, but one must go with Zechariah.

The second beast *"exerciseth"* all the power ofthefust beast and *"causeth"* the earth to worship the first beast. He can cause great wonders to be done, such as fire coming down out of heaven. Now guess what that fire is. Is it some Star Wars technology? It could be. Do you remember in chapter 6 that there would be falling stars? Do you reckon that these stars could actually be Satan's angels putting on a show? Well, you should, because that is one of the things they can do. Satan will deceive so impressively that a bewildered, self-centered mankind will readily follow him, and besides, the Beast can't be killed. And look at what will happen if one doesn't follow—death.

He will cause an image, a replica of the first beast, to be made. Do you think it to beflesh-like? Remember, there is cloning. Do you think it to be indwelled by a demon? Absolutely.

So, what do we have here, a trinity? Yes. We have one that cannot be killed. Also, we have one that worships and demands that others do the same. And we have a manufactured job that is equally powerful. Revelation 6:4 is beginning co roll.To a foolish mankind, who better to follow?

Remember who is in control of the food supply. Aha! Then we must be seeing Revelation 6:5f. People will follow as long as the leader has the purse strings in his control. The Beast, the Satan- indwelled Antichrist, has a good show going on, and there is no one causing him problems. I believe that Satan will use demons in verse 8 of chapter 6 to help kill more people. The Antichrist has a stranglehold on the world, and his kingdom will do whatever he says. By being forced, yes, but as we will see later, so very willingly.

There is so very much encouragement in that last verse, you know, the one of 666. You ask me if I'm nuts, and I say no. You see, this also is a hidden message to the believers, that the one who holds this 666 is just a created being. Man was created on the sixth day. The Trinity wanted to state that this person is just a created being.

This person is not a true god and will certainly be *judged.* Someone (the Beast of the first half of the tribulation) will boastfully hold that number, not knowing it is a mark of doom. When I finally saw that, I sure did rejoice. So mud1fuss has been sent up in the air about the number and the person who will hold it. But take courage—the Creator is in control of this *one* also.

Daniel 7:24–27 reads:

> *24. And the ten horns out of this kingdom are ten kings that shall arise: and another shall rise after them; and he shall be diverse from the first, and he shall subdue three kings.*
> *25. And he shall speak great words against the most High, and shall wear out the saints of the most High, and think to change times and laws: and they shall be given into his hand until a time and times and the dividing of time.*
> *26. But the judgment shall sit, and they shall take away his dominion, to consume and to destroy it unto the end.*
> *27. And the kingdom and dominion, and the greatness of the kingdom under the whole heaven, shall be given to the people of the saints of the most High, whose kingdom is an everlasting kingdom, and all dominions shall serve and obey him.*

Daniel 7:25 shows the intent and vigor of the one, 666; however, verse 26 straightens this misconception out in a hurry:

"But the judgment shall sit." You see, folks, the last six chapters of Daniel show the game plan of both sides in the battle of Revelation. Now consider this next point, please.

Let's look at this fearsome one, 666. Read Daniel 7:8–14:

> 8. I considered the horns, and, behold, there came up among them another little horn, before whom there were three of the first horns plucked up by the roots: and, behold, in this horn were eyes like the eyes of man, and a mouth speaking great things.
>
> 9. I beheld till the thrones were cast down, and the ancient of days did sit, whose garment was white as snow, and the hair of his head like the pure wool: his throne was like the fiery flame, and his wheels as burning fire.
>
> 10. A fiery stream issued and came forth from before him: thousand thousands ministered unto him, and ten thousand times ten thousand stood before him: the judgment was set, and the books were opened.
>
> 11. I beheld then because of the voice of the great words which the horn spake: I beheld even rill the beast was slain, and his body destroyed, and given to the burning flame.
>
> 12. As concerning the rest of the beasts, they had their dominion taken away: yet their lives were prolonged for a season and time.
>
> 13. I saw in the night visions, and, behold, one like the Son of man came with the clouds of heaven, and came to the Ancient of days, and they brought him near before him.
>
> 14. And there was given him dominion, and glory, and a kingdom, that all people, nations, and languages, should serve him: his dominion is an everlasting dominion, which shall not pass away, and his kingdom that which shall not be destroyed.

One can clearly see what will happen at the end of the tribulation period, including the end of the thousand-year reign, and who is going to be making the decisions. We see, since He knows what is going to happen, He must be the one who brings about His will. Lucifer is such a dope; he doesn't want to openly accept that he is a puppet.

Now you can see why I said that the 666 of verse 18 is a hidden message of encouragement to the believers during that time. Will many lose their lives at the whim of evil? Sad to say, but yes, they will. You did see the hint of verse 11.

Here again is the heritage Adam left us. Do not get indignant toward Adam; just look at our failures. Is this our nature? Yes, as God explains in Genesis 6. However, if God had somehow seen to it that the choice made it all the way down to our time of being on this earth, one of us would have chosen wrongly. We *know* to do right, and more importantly the *consequences,* but as Paul explains in Romans 7, that's not the choice we make. Adam knew to do right and chose wrong; do we actually think we would do better?

Chapter 14

1. And I looked, and, lo, a Lamb stood on the mount Sion, and with him an hundred forty and four thousand, having his Father's name written in their foreheads.

2. And I heard a voice from heaven, as the voice of many waters, and as the voice of a great thunder: and I heard the voice of harpers harping with their harps:

3. And they sung as it were a new song before the throne, and before the four beasts, and the elders: and no man could learn that song but the hundred and forty and four thousand, which were redeemed from the earth.

4. These are they which were not defiled with women; for they are virgins. These are they which fallow the Lamb whithersoever he goeth. These were redeemed from among men, being the first fruits unto God and to the Lamb.

5. And in their mouth was found no guile: for they are without fault before the throne of God.

We see the Lord has lost none of the sealed, just as He said of all those who are His in the Gospel of John, chapter 17. He and they are standing in a place of power. In the Bible, mountains represent power, and especially Mount Sion. We hear from heaven a sound of commendation and celebration, and we hear the unmistakable sounds of acclamation. The Lamb and the Holy Spirit are accomplishing the job of bringing evil to an end. The new song is the setting up of a new era. Do I hear a "what?"

There has to be an end for there to be a beginning:

a. Satan and his forces are following their desires.

b. Their path will lead downward, because anything that is evil goes down.

c. The Lord has but to start judging, and it is soon coming.

d. The Lord's word is being accomplished, and that always means victory.

e. Satan's forces always defile and lessen.

f. The Lord's forces are worthy and without fault.

The voice as a great thunder is the proclamation of acceptance. Do you remember it being said *"This is my beloved Son"* (Matt. 3:17)? Did I hear an amen?

The personages being finished, but God wanting to finish the *encouragement* to the saints of this period, He then installs chapter 14. Juse as chapter 6 is used to outline the Book of Revelation, God uses chapters 12-15 to map the second half. It will be such a difficult time for one and all. However, God's attention (encouragement) is toward His children. We think our life is difficult in these times, and they are, but not nearly what these folks are going to see.

Remember, the seventh trumpet sounded, signaling the start of the second half of the tribulation. We've seen the ark, which is the presence of God, but it also means the righteousness of God is realized or brought co the front. Look at these points:

Chapter 12 introduces the players, if you will, of the tribulation.

Chapter 13 shows the existence and the game plan of Satan and his kingdom.

Chapter 14 shows the power, position, and reward of God's forces, and His plan.

Chapter 15 shows the temple scene of the glory of the saved (saints) of the last half of the tribulation. Living by faith does not require sight; *we just need to keep moving.*

In chapter 14, the first thing we see is the futuristic picture of Christ standing on Mount Sion, which is the government of the nation. Could it mean the Mount of Olives? Yes, it is part of the mount of God. When He puts His feet on the Mount of Olives, it will cleave into two sides. From there, He goes on to the battle of Armageddon. This is also the time of His setting up of His government, His rule on earth.

> *6. And I saw another angel fly in the midst of heaven, having the everlasting gospel to preach unto them that dwell on the earth, and to every nation, and kindred, and tongue, and people,*
> *7. Saying with a Loud voice, Fear God, and give glory to him; for the hour of his judgment is come: and worship him that made heaven, and earth, and the sea, and the fountains of waters.*

This chapter could be called the loud chapter; God is going to hold nothing back when He starts His judgments. No one will be able to say, "Well, God, I didn't hear Your last call to repent. I didn't know You were coming." In these two verses, God Himself publishes a salvation message. Glory!

You must realize that the harsh efforts of the Antichrist have been established, and everything is coordinated with the mark.

Before God really gets moving in this, the second half of the tribulation, He issues a call of salvation. But let's look at the scope of that call. You would think a call to the earth would be sufficient; God goes much further than that. He rakes it down from the nations to kindreds (nationalities), then to tongues (languages), and then to people (to tribes and such). Psalm 22, the suffering messianic psalm, mentions this. Look there in verses 2–28: *"All the ends of the world shall remember and turn unto the Lord: and all the kindreds of the nations shall worship before thee. For the kingdom is the LORD's: and he is the governor among the nations."*

God will have those that will turn to Him. Does this mean that all will get saved? No, they will hear, some will accept, but the rest will be without excuse. It's kinda like the seed on the wayside. Every knee will bow to Christ one time or another.

This angel will accomplish his job of preaching. Oh, that we would ours!

His message is to fear the right person-not a created being, but the eternal God. The Lord said it best in Matthew 10:26–28:

> *26. Fear them not therefore: for there is nothing covered, that shall not be revealed; and hid, that shall not be known.*
> *27. What I tell you in darkness, that speak ye in light: and what ye hear in the ear, that preach ye upon the housetops.*
> *28. And fear not them which kill the body, but are not able to kill the soul: but rather fear him which is able to destroy both soul and body in hell.*

The folks of the second half will know all too well the reality of these verses and the total seriousness of this last clause. Oh, dear Lord!

Some will also understand the importance and the personal pleasure of glorifying Him. *This is something we take for granted* Silly us–we sit in our easy chairs and complain and pray a halfhearted prayer. Boy, these folks will deserve the special place they will receive.

The people of the earth will live the judgment of Him who made heaven (the power that hovers above them), the earth (that shakes beneath), the sea (that once was productive for food), and the water (a life-sustaining necessity). God's message is short and to the point. He is giving mankind a choice: be evil, or turn to God. They see the mark, on one hand; and on the other, they hear the preaching angel. On the one hand, they can commit to God and have an eternal hope, expecting harm in this life but in the end attaining heaven, or they can continue the way they are going. You know, to them, it adds up to harm anyway they go about it. Where would we place om eyes? Where have you placed yom eyes? Boy, now we can see the true reality of faith. They will be in quite a pickle.

> *8. And there followed another angel saying, Babylon is fallen, is fallen, that great city, because she made all nations drink of the wine of the wrath of her fornication.*

105

As I said, God is showing His outline of what is going to take place. Right after the Mount Sion scene and the angel preaching the gospel, God gets down to business. He is forecasting the doom of the evil kingdom. It has not happened yet in the book; He is letting His suffering people know what is about to happen. Guess what? I would like to cover this verse better, but I want to save this glorious victory for chapter 17. As I said before, it will be worth it. I want to give you the real good stuff on these evil things all at one time.

> 9. *And the third angel fallowed them, saying with a loud voice, If any man worship the beast and his image, and receive his mark in his forehead, or in his hand,*
> 10.*The same shall drink of the wine of the wrath of God, which is poured out without mixture into the cup of his indignation; and he shall be tormented with fire and brimstone in the presence of the holy angels, and in the presence of the Lamb:*
> 11. *And the smoke of their torment ascendeth up far ever and ever: and they have no rest day nor night, who worship the beast and his image, and whosoever receiveth the mark of his name.*
> 12. *Here is the patience of the saints: here are they that keep the commandments of God, and the faith of Jesus.*

These folks of verses –11 have made the wrong choice. They chose to worship the created instead of the Creator. They chose to accept his identifying mark in their person. This mark shows ownership. Since there is onlyone Creator, He and He alone has the position of ownership.

To give mankind something to focus on, God uses the word *"cup."* Their drinking water has already been touched; what better vehicle could be used than the very thing that they must have water. God uses the words *"wine of the wrath"* in order to give another focus point; that is, their deeds (evil) will be scrutinized and will return unto them in theform of a bitter drink-so much so that they *"shall be tormented with fire and brimstone,"* and their torment shall be supervised by the Lord and His angels.

Then look at this neat thing: *"The smoke of their torment ascendeth up far ever and ever:and they have no rest day nor night, who worship the beast and his image, and whosoever receiveth the mark of his name."* Neat, in that righteousness is not being held back. Oh, it is sad but true that mankind's decisions have consequences.

These worshipers may think that since this beast came out of the bottomless pit, fire won't hurt them. Where there is smoke, there is fire. Fire means the breaking down of components, and yet their torment is forever; therefore, there will be great suffering. Since it is forever, they cannot be consumed and will suffer and suffer. God did the creating; therefore, He should be able to make it possible for them to suffer with no escape and die for all eternity. Do we remember something being said about the last laugh in our culture today? I weep at the thought of those who won't turn.

> 13. And I heard a voice from heaven saying unto me, Write, Blessed are the dead which die in the Lord from henceforth: Yea, saith the Spirit, that they may rest from their labours; and their works do follow them.

God rewards faith; we will see the special position that these folks will have later in the book. The key point to realize is that God understands suffering and faith and works that follow; in other words, works of real faith, and He will never owe anyone anything. Here he wants these tribulation saints and us to know ahead of time that He will respond in a most honorable way. They will have a blessed rest, and in *His presence.* God is so righteous and so good.

> 14. And I looked, and behold a white cloud, and upon the cloud one sat like unto the Son of man, having on his head a golden crown, and in his hand a sharp sickle.

> 15. And another angel came out of the temple, crying with
> a loud voice to him that sat on the cloud, Thrust in thy
> sickle, and reap:for the time iscome for thee to reap;
> for the harvest of the earth is ripe.
> 16. And he that sat on the cloud thrust in his sickle on the
> earth; and the earth was reaped.

Of course, this is the Judge, the Lord Jesus Christ. He is wearing a crown, showing His deity, and holding a sharp sickle, showing His authority and action. Yes, but He is waiting to thrust in His sickle. Remember that this chapter is a preview of the coming events of the last half of the tribulation. Thus far the tribulation has followed the Book of Daniel and must continue to do so in order to becorrect. It is written in this way to show the outline, yes; however, it still has the purpose of encouragement to the righteous of that time and to us.

One thing to point out here is, where do you think the blood on the vesture came from that the Lord wears in chapter 19? Oops—I'm getting ahead of myself. Remember, Jehovah Sabaoth is the commander-in-chief of the forces.

> 17. And another angel came out of the temple which is in
> heaven, he also having a sharp sickle.
> 18. And another angel came out from the altar, which had
> power over fire; and cried with a loud cry to him that
> had the sharp sickle, saying, Thrust in thy sharp sickle,
> and gather the clusters of the vine of the earth; for her
> grapes are fully ripe.
> 19. And the angel thrust in his sickle into the earth, and
> gathered the vine of the earth, and cast it into thegreat
> winepress of the wrath of God
> 20. And the wine press was trodden without the city, and blood
> came out of the wine press, even unto the horse bridles, by
> the space of a thousand and six hundred furlongs.

Please notice the use of the words "clusters" and "vine." Here God is showing that more than just individuals, but nations, are intended. God is showing us the end of this evil world and world system. Then God uses grapes to designate individuals and small groups; the key point is their unbelief. Every soul we point to Christ now, if they get saved, will not go through these things.

One cannot serve God in unbelief. The word *Armageddon* is not mentioned here, but the view is of that battle. Here again, God is giving encouragement to us and to the saved people of this period. He is exposing His plan.

The angel coming from the altar and having power over fire is not an accident. Oftentimes when grain fields are harvested, the stubble is burned to get ready for the next crop. It also puts ash back into the soil, which is a great fertilizer. The biggest thing to think about is that many times the Lord Himself mentioned that unbelievers would suffer in eternal burning. Can we show mercy?

If we stop and think just a minute, Lucifer has to have read this or heard it; it looks like he would try to keep these things from happening. His march to his doom is getting shorter and shorter.

Chapter 15

1. And I saw another sign in heaven, great and marvellous, seven angels having the seven last plagues; for in them is filled up the wrath of God.

2. And I saw as it were a sea of glass mingled with fire: and them that had gotten the victory over the beast, and over his image, and over his mark, and over the number of his name, stand on the sea of glass, having the harps of God.

3. And they sing the song of Moses the servant of God, and the song of the Lamb, saying, Great and marvellous are thy works, Lord God Almighty; just and true are thy ways, thou King of saints.

4. Who shall not fear thee, 0 Lord, and glorify thy name? for thou only art holy: for all nations shall come and worship before thee; for thy judgments are made manifest.

This scene is still in the preview before God starts His judgments. You might say, but how, since verse 1 and verse 5 are so closely the same. The words *"And I saw another sign"* set the scene for us to see the last thing to view before God starts the destruction. The last verse of chapter 11 and verse 5 of this chapter fit together.

One more thing to see is that the events of verses 1-4 have not occurred. They are still future. These folks have gotten victory over the Beast, and over his image and his mark. They are standing on the sea of glass; the same laver or sea of glass of chapter 4. Notice also that it is mingled with fire; fire is judgment, and the laver was a place of cleansing. God promises in the Old Testament that this period will be the worst trial the earth has ever seen. These verses picture their suffering time here on earth and the position they will have in the thousand-year reign.

These verses and 7:14ff show the horrendous time of these folks who are on this sea *"mingled with fire."* Here again, God is encouraging His saints with the knowledge of what will happen before it happens, showing them their reward. God is letting us know that only He is in control.

Think about it, folks. The believers who are mentioned in the last part of chapter 11 of Hebrews are also called faithful. Yet they did not have the same ending as those mentioned in the first part of that same chapter. What section will your life and my life fir into? Will our faith be such that we will deserve mentioning? Yes, I'm glad that church age believers won't see these times.

It is a beautiful song they sing and seems a bit of an invitation, wouldn't you agree? The folks during this time period can look to the one who is being praised as someone worthy of praise. Words like *"marvellous ... works," "Lord God Almighty," "true ... ways" "King," "fear thee," "glorify," "holy," "worship," "Judgments,"* and *"manifest"* all point to believing in one who is the winner.

Now let's look at something. Chapter 11:19 says, *"And the temple of God was opened in heaven, and there was seen in his temple the ark of his testament: and there were lightnings, and voices, and thunderings, and an earthquake, and great hail."* Now let's put our next text with it:

> 5. *And after that I looked, and, behold, the temple of the tabernacle of the testimony in heaven was opened:*
> 6. *And the seven angels came out of the temple, having the seven plagues, clothed in pure and white linen, and having their breasts girded with golden girdles.*
> 7. *And one of the four beasts gave unto the seven angels seven golden vials full of the wrath of God, who liveth for ever and ever.*
> 8. *And the temple was filled with smoke from the glory of God, and from his power; and no man was able to enter into the temple, till the seven plagues of the seven angels were fulfilled.*

Now we have the initiation of the events God is going to make happen in the last half of the tribulation period. As we saw in chapter 11, the temple was opened and the ark was seen, and then *"there were lightnings, and voices, and thunderings, and an earthquake, and great hail."* Is there a rhythm to God's use of *"there were lightnings, and voices, and thunderings"?* It seems that each time it is used in this book, something is added to the phrase. God is just doing a thorough job.

Now, in verse 5, the temple is opened. First the ark is seen (the testimony is available); the righteousness of that testimony requires action. there is sent out of the throne seven angels. Notice that one of the four beasts gave the vials of wrath; the four beasts represent the Lord Jesus. The righteous wrath of God is finally being poured onto the deserving recipients. Remember, too, in chapter 14, that the cup of the whore and God's cup of wrath are used. Now, in these verses, God uses vials (cups).

One should understand from these verses that God does require justice, and it is thorough. Remember, there is a time of grace and a time of judgment.

Because of the shekinah glory of God, no man is able to approach the holy God wuil the judgment is finished. There will be no movement in or out of the temple until God has accomplished His purpose. these angels are dressed in white (holiness) and have on golden girdles (having to do with the throne). Let's look at one last thing.

God is totally committed to what is about to happen. He has fulfilled holiness. He has fulfilled all requirements of righteousness toward His entire creation. It is all systems go, but please don't miss the heart of God, as seen in Matthew 10:28–33:

> 28. *And fear not them which kill the body, but are not able to kill the soul: but rather fear him which is able to destroy both soul and body in hell.*
> 29. *Are not two sparrows sold for a farthing? and one of them shall not fall on the ground without your Father.*

30. But the very hairs of your head are all numbered

31. Fear ye not therefore, ye are of more value than many sparrows.

32. Whosoever therefore shall confess me before men, him will I confess also before my Father which is in heaven.

33. But whosoever shall deny me before men, him will I also deny before my Father which is in heaven.

The shekinah glory of God is seen because of the detrimental effects of sin on His creation. His whole creation has had to suffer, and as we saw above, He suffers. Oh, the hurt of God! Oh, the heart of God! Please don't miss that when Jesus hung on the cross with all the effects of sin placed on Him, and the Father and the Holy Spirit turned from Christ, they too had to be in such agony. Is it possible they are the ones who tore the veil?

With tears in my eyes, I say that we overlook the pain that God has gone through and is going through and will go through. Does God feel hurt, or is He grieved when a tragedy happens? Yes, He created mankind and all there is. As Hebrews 2:17-18 says, *"Wherefore in all things it behoved him to be made Like unto his brethren, that he might be a merciful and faithful high priest in things pertaining to God, to make reconciliation for the sins of the people. For in that he himself hath suffered being tempted, he is able to succour them that are tempted."*

In all points, He suffered the pains of mankind. He cried in the garden. Our hurts are an additional hurt to what He already feels. Millions of mankind's ranks have gone to hell, and He watches each one.

Millions of his animals have been offered in order to fulfill the ordinances of His offerings, and He was always there. Those offerings were put in place to show mankind that sin costs. And still it hurts.

For mankind to be with God, sin had to be judged. It hurt the Lord Jesus Christ to endure the trial and to be crucified.

So, when you read that the temple was so engulfed in smoke that no man was able to enter the temple, remember that God has hurt and will hurt. In chapter 21, when He wipes away our tears, will He also be wiping away His? I know He cares.

Chapter 16

*1. And I heard a great voice out of the temple saying to the
seven angels, Go your ways, and pour out the vials of the
wrath of God upon the earth.*

Noticing that no one isseen, one should easily see the ending
of chapter 11 and the last part of chapter 15. The intent, in my
opinion, is to focus on the open ark, the smoke-filled temple (the
shekinah glory), and the intense activity of a holy God against evil.

God and His creation have had to put up with the fall and
activity of Satan and his crowd. Now it is time to judge as only
God can. You did notice that the voice is described as great, and
you do remember chapter 1.

*2. And the first went, and poured out his vial upon the earth;
and there fell a noisome and grievous sore upon the men
which had the mark of the beast, and upon them which
worshipped his image.*

Yeehaw, go get 'em, God! I can't imagine what the godly
are going through, but I can imagine them needing some
encouragement. Look at it: Satan is rolling along, as well as all
of his followers. Then God interrupts the scene with sores. Hey,
who's in charge here?

*3. And the second angel poured out his vial upon the sea; and
it became as the blood of a dead man: and every living
soul died in the sea. [All of God's sea creation had to die.]*

God gave them a taste of this in chapter 8. Now it looks like someone is really upsetting the cart. Think of the devastation and the stink. Maybe the 'in' crowd is not in charge after all. What do you think of the food supply now? What do you think of commerce now? What do you think of the movement of goods now? When God, in 11:17, took His power and the elders praised Him for it, do you think the world had any idea what was about to happen? Yeah, me neither.

> 4. And the third angel poured out his vial upon the rivers and fountains of waters; and they became blood.
> 5. And I heard the angel of the waters say, Thou art righteous, O Lord, which art, and wast, and shalt be, because thou hast judged thus.
> 6. For they have shed the blood of saints and prophets, and thou hast given them blood to drink; for they are worthy.
> 7. And I heard another out of the altar say, Even so, Lord God Almighty, true and righteous are thy judgments.

Okay, what will they do if they have no water to drink? Touching their ability to move goods and to make money is one thing, but to take a life source like water away, that is just cruel. Who does this God think He is, to pull such a stunt? After all, the all-powerful one who can kill and not be killed said to take the mark because *he* was in charge of this world. Aha—*not anymore!*

While hanging on the cross, the Lord said, *"I thirst"* in John, the nineteenth chapter. I wonder if this crowd remembers what their ancestors did then? Does God need to hear verses 5–7? No, but when these events happen, unrighteous mankind will have no recourse. The angels stayed back while the Lord hung on the cross. Now they can say, *"True and righteous are thy judgments."* From righteous Abel to the time of these verses, the ground has had to accept the blood of God's people and all of mankind. Oh, the last laugh is harsh for those that ain't laughing!

> 8. And the fourth angel poured out his vial upon the sun; and power was given unto him to scorch men with fire.

> *9. And men were scorched with great heat, and blasphemed the name of God, which hath power over these plagues: and they repented not to give him glory.*

I personally think that God's actions in the second half are toward the latter part of the period. The reason is this: I don't think man can survive as well against His actions. I don't find a particular time given, and I personally think these events will be in rapid succession.

What man has seen is the unparalleled audacity and cruelty of the Beast. Consequently, millions have gotten saved, and millions have died Now the 'in' crowd has to deal with the righteous God.

We find also that He uses the sun in this instance. Remember what was said about the ones listed at the end of chapter 7, that the sun would not harm them anymore. The great tribulation saints will have to endure the elements. The goods of this world will be controlled by the Beast. The godly will be hunted by man and demon. Here, God is using the same sun to harm the harmers, so to speak. Verse 9 shows the stubbornness of mankind; it must be a thing that instead of repentance, one should hold on to evil. Do we not see this in our lives today?

> *10. And the fifth angel poured out his vial upon the seat of the beast; and his kingdom was full of darkness; and they gnawed their tongues for pain,*
> *11. And blasphemed the God of heaven because of their pains and their sores, and repented not of their deeds.*

Now evil mankind has gone from too much sun (you reckon they got a good tan) to no sun at all, and this is one of the things they've worshiped for thousands of years. Now, God, is that poetic justice? Take a good look at us (man). Instead of repenting and turning to God, we would rather bite ourselves to have something to focus on. My, we are so intelligent.

> *12. And the sixth angel poured out his vial upon the great river Euphrates; and the water there of was dried up, that the way of the kings of the east might be prepared.*

Will the Beast have great control over the Asian nations? That is a very good question. What hardware will they have for battle? And why will a river have to be dried up so they can get into the coming battle? Has the empowered Beast had trouble getting these nations in line? Will it be the easiest way to get that much manpower across the river? The Oriental nations were not part of the old Roman Empire.

The forces of the northern kingdoms and the southern kingdoms will be the focal point during this period. However, this part of the world will not be left out, and consider the billions of people there today. After all, God is judging the entire world, so this is a world gathering that is coming.

> *13. And I saw three unclean spirits like frogs come out of the mouth of the dragon, and out of the mouth of the beast, and out of the mouth of the false prophet.*
>
> *14. For they are the spirits of devils, working miracles, which go forth unto the kings of the earth and of the whole world, to gather them to the battle of that great day of God Almighty.*
>
> *15. Behold, I come as a thief Blessed is he that watcheth, and keepeth his garments, lest he walk naked, and they see his shame.*
>
> *16. And he gathered them together into a place called in the Hebrew tongue Armageddon.*

Uh-oh! These verses are self-explanatory. Please note where these spirits come from and the power they will have to persuade. In this instance, God uses evil itself to accomplish His will. Satan thinks he is accomplishing something special; however, God accomplishes His will instead.

Satan has to be thinking that if he can get all these folks in one spot, God's people won't have a chance, and that will mean God doesn't have a chance. Remember the last verse of chapter 12. He sure is a funny. Because of the tragedy of it all, no one can laugh.

17. And the seventh angel poured out his vial into the air; and there came a great voice out of the temple of heaven, from the throne, saying, It is done.

18. And there were voices, and thunders, and lightnings; and there was a great earthquake, such as was not since men were upon the earth, so mighty an earthquake, and so great.

19. And the great city was divided into three parts, and the cities of the nation fell: and great Babylon came in remembrance before God, to give unto her the cup of the wine of the fierceness of his wrath.

20. And every island fled away, and the mountains were not found.

21. And there fell upon men a great hail out of heaven, every stone about the weight of a talent: and men blasphemed God because of the plague of the hail for the plague thereof was exceeding great.

Do you remember reading in the Gospel of John that the Lord said, *"It is finished"*? The Lord says here, *"It is done."* The Lord will always have the last laugh. Boy, and then in verse 18 come the voices, thunders, lightnings, and a great earthquake. Please remember that the temple is still engulfed in the smoke from the shekinah glory. *Get 'em, God!*

In verse 19, while God is gathering the nations to the battlefield, He gives them something to think about. Jerusalem is divided by an earthquake (11:8, *"the great city"*), and the structures (buildings) fall in the cities. Then the world's religious center itself becomes God's focus. We are about to deal with her, so be patient.

In verse 20, we are caught up to the outline of Revelation 6:14. While verse 20 brings us to 6:15f, what is seen in 16:20 is what is revealed in chapters 17 and 18. You see, there were so many questions chat just haunted me until God brought His outline into view. Now I can see His sequence of events. Now we get to some really good stuff, not chat the other wasn't good. I just had more questions than I knew what to do with.

An important thing to remember is that evil mankind, even seeing the mountains and the islands taken away, would rather be annihilated with rocks than turn to God. Now, how petty is evil?

What did the Lord say about faith and the removal of mountains? In my life, there have been times that God has touched my heart, but He really is getting serious with these folks.

God is now going to break the action in order to give us some information of grave concern in chapter 17.

Chapter 17

This chapter is a very exciting chapter. Its information about evil is rich beyond belief. This chapter is an explanatory chapter of the Beast and his religious system. It is a prelude to chapter 18. It shows just how God can get us to do what He wants, and we thought it was our idea all along. Think of NAFTA and some of those other world agreements that have hurt so much. Mankind is in charge of itself ... or is it? God, as He did with Pharoah, knows just how to get our unbelieving hides to do what He wants. All the while, He will help us do for Him what we want to do for Him, as long as it is in His will.

1. *And there came one of the seven angels which had the seven vials, and talked with me, saying unto me, Come hither; I will shew unto thee the judgment of the great whore that sitteth upon many waters:*
2. *With whom the kings of the earth have committed fornication, and the inhabitants of the earth have been made drunk with the wine of her fornication.*
3. *So he carried me away in the spirit into the wilderness: and I saw a woman sit upon a scarlet coloured beast, full of names of blasphemy, having seven heads and ten horns.*
4. *And the woman was arrayed in purple and scarlet colour, and decked with gold and precious stones and pearls, having a golden cup in her hand full of abominations and filthiness of her fornication:*
5. *And upon her forehead was a name written, MYSTERY, BABYLON THE GREAT, THE MOTHER OF HARLOTS AND ABOMINATIONS OF THE EARTH*

6. *And I saw the woman drunken with the blood of the saints, and with the blood of the martyrs of Jesus: and when I saw her, I wondered with great admiration.*

7. *And the angel said unto me, Wherefore didst thou marvel? I will tell thee the mystery of the woman, and of the beast that carrieth he,: which hath the seven heads and ten horns.*

Man's basic belief, driving mentality, way of life, and commitment to life are personified by this woman. A female, a whore, is used because the true and living God, the Creator, is the one being cheated on. He only goes by He, not It or She. Well, you ask, how can this be an adulterous lifestyle? I am sure glad you asked.

1. *Our commitment to do what we want to do, without a care as to the requirements of the Creator—A woman starts it off, and a willful man jumps right in. Read Genesis 3:2–13:*

2. *And the woman said unto the serpent, We may eat of the fruit of the trees of the garden:*

3. *But of the fruit of the tree which is in the midst of the garden, God hath said, Ye shall note at of it, neither shall ye touch it, lest ye die.*

4. *And the serpent said unto the woman, Ye shall not surely die:*

5. *For God doth know that in the day ye eat thereof, then your eyes shall be opened, and ye shall be as gods, knowing good and evil*

6. *And when the woman saw that the tree was good for food, and that it was pleasant to the eyes, and a tree to be desired to make one wise, she took of the fruit thereof, and did eat,. and gave also unto her husband with her; and he did eat.*

7. *And the eyes of them both were opened, and they knew that they were naked; and they sewed fig leaves together, and made themselves aprons.*

8. *And they heard the voice of the Lord God walking in the garden in the cool of the day:and Adam and his*

wife hid themselves from the presence of the Lord God amongst the trees of the garden.

9. And the Lord God called unto Adam, and said unto him, Where art thou?

10. And he said, I heard thy voice in the garden, and I was afraid, because I was naked; and I hid myself

11. And he said, Who told thee that thou wast naked? Hast thou eaten of the tree, whereof I commanded thee that thou shouldest not eat?

12. And the man said, The woman whom thou gavest to be with me, she gave me of the tree, and I did eat.

13. And the Lord God said unto the woman, What is this that thou hast done? And the woman said, The serpent beguiled me, and I did eat.

Satan's decision to contact Eve first is easily seen as to why in 2 Timothy 2:26. Down through the ages, the following have been seen:

1. The man of the species wants things easy, and not to have to take responsibility, which is the very place God put him into. He was to take care of the garden and to multiply throughout the entire world.
2. The female does not want to follow as God said for her to do. She does not want to be ruled; chapter 18 will show this even greater.

Just a thought here, neither male nor female of the human race, the very ones that was created in God's image, easily accepts being ruled. We are engulfed in a treacherous heart that has to be captured by wills.

We see from these verses concerning Adam and Eve the following:

a. She added to the word of God to satisfy or bolster self or self's image (v. 3).

b. She saw supply, pleasantness, helpfulness. She reasoned out its qualities, and that they should be used (v. 6).

c. She decided that since it would make her wise, she has every right to make her own decision.

d. She incorporated someone to be in the sin with her (v. 6).

e. They decided one should not face up to their sin and the consequences of it, instead cover it up and hope it goes away. Most importantly, just don't take responsibility for it (v. 7).

f. First things first, hide. This is still not taking responsibility for sin (v. 8).

g. Admit to only what you have to (v. 10).

h. Cause the blame to be shifted to someone else (v. 12f).

Adam knew that what Eve had done was wrong, but he was completely willing to try it. Boy, does that not exemplify mankind all through the ages, serve self, get others to serve them, expect others to serve them.

Mankind ended up fighting the very world that had been created for its pleasure. All the while, man was being stalked by death. Does anyone remember the fourth horse and its rider?

We also see an *enhancement* of Adam and Eve's approach to life. It will show the polishing that mankind has given to *its* rights.

3. Our commitment to act and bring about our will, our rights—In 1 Kings 21:–15, we see the assumption of right or the possession of a right:

5. But Jezebel his wife came to him, and said unto him, Why is thy spirit so sad, that thou eatest no bread?

6. And he said unto her, Because I spake unto Naboth the Jezreelite, and said unto him, Give me thy vineyard for money; or else, if it please thee, I will give thee another vineyard for it: and he answered, I will not give thee my vineyard.

7. And Jezebel his wife said unto him, Dost thou now govern the kingdom of Israel? arise, and eat bread, and let thine eart be merry: I will give thee the vineyard of Naboth the Jezreelite.

8. So she wrote letters in Ahab's name, and sealed them with his seal, and sent the letters unto the elders and to the nobles that were in his city, dwelling with Naboth.

9. And she wrote in the letters, saying, Proclaim a fast, and set Naboth on high among the people:

10. And set two men, sons of Belial before him, to bear witness against him, saying, Thou didst blaspheme God and the king. And then carry him out, and stone him, that he may die.

11. And the men of his city, even the eklers and the nobles who were the inhabitants in his city, did as Jezebel had sent unto them, and as it was written in the letters which she had sent unto them.

12. They prodaimed a fast, and set Naboth on high among the people.

13. And there came in two men, children of Belia!, and sat before him: and the men of Belia! witnessed against him, even against Naboth, in the presence of the people, saying, Naboth did blaspheme God and the king. Then they carried him forth out of the city, and stoned him with stones, that he died.

14. Then they sent to Jezebel, saying, Naboth is stoned, and is dead.

15. And it came to pass, when Jezebel heard that Naboth was stoned, and was dead, that Jezebel said to Ahab, Arise, take possession of the vineyard of Naboth the Jezreelite, which he refused to give thee for money: for Naboth is not alive, but dead.

What are the traits that we see displayed in this passage?

a. We see the assertion of one's own worth, and the right to exercise their abilities because of that worth to get their way (v. 7)

b. We see a willingness to deceive by use of others or their position (v. 8).

c. There is also the use of others to get your will done. Do what you want and hope for the best (vv. 9-13).

d. We see a coldness to the hurt or hurting of others (v. 15).

The perpetrators ended up being cursed because of their actions and hunted by death (fulfilled in later chapters), as were Adam and Eve.

All that was gained in both cases was lost, and disgrace, depravity, and death were the end result.

When adultery is committed, the relationship has ceased to be. The only way that the relationship can be reestablished is for forgiveness to take place, along with a commitment to fidelity and the injured party trusting that fidelity. This is the very picture of salvation from God:

 a. The payment of forgiveness was the death of the Lord on the cross. God Himself and Adam's spirit were separated by sin; hence, Adam's spirit was dead because all of life is with God.

 b. Adam, now being encapsulated by sin, could not effect fidelity; hence, Adam and all from Adam must die a physical death.

 c. When drawn by the Holy Spirit, a believer's spirit, at the moment of repentance and turning to God for salvation, will be indwelled by the Holy Spirit and will be sealed until the day of redemption.

It should be easy to see why the Lord calls this system a whore—anything for self, no matter the cost.

It is little wonder why the Lord is praised in 16:5–7:

 5. And I heard the angel of the waters say, Thou art righteous, 0 Lord, which art, and wast, and shalt be, because thou hast judged thus.

 6. For they have shed the blood of saints and prophets, and thou hast given them blood to drink; for they are worthy.

 7. And I heard another out of the altar say, Even so, Lord God Almighty, true and righteous are thy judgments.

Sin has to be judged before man can have peace with God.

So, considering the characteristics, would you say the great whore has the following characteristics:

1. A commitment to self only
2. A commitment to do whatever it takes to get her way
3. A commitment to please self, as seen Revelation 18:7: *"How much she hath glorified herself, and lived deliciously, so much torment and sorrow give her: for she saith in her heart, I sit a queen, and am no widow, and shall see no sorrow."*

In Genesis 10:8-10, viewing the life of Nimrod, we will find these characteristics polished to perfection.

In verse 1 of our text, we find that sin must be judged. Heretofore, we have seen this self-gratifying philosophy of life rest on all mankind's waters. This chapter and chapter 18 will reinforce this. Remember, *"water"* or *"waters"* as used in Revelation 13: 1 represent mankind.

In verse 2, we find that the rulers of this world do not want to be held accountable and will readily embrace this way of life. It also says that the inhabitants of the world have become drunk with the wine of her fornication. Mankind wants to promote itself, and the verse's use of the word *"wine"* is significant. In 14:8, we see *"the wine of the wrath of her fornication."* The evil of mankind, such as seen in the two scriptures of Genesis 6 and 1 Kings, is best exemplified by *"the wine of the wrath of her fornication."* Just as Adam and Eve did not want to be told what to do, so evil, with a vengeance, does not want anyone or anything to interfere with the fulfilling of its desires.

1. Fornication = evil desires; no desire to be righteous or obey
2. Wrath= commitment to not be supervised or to not give an account to God
3. Wine= actions= lifestyle

The Antichrist has made such an organization of debauchery, a home base, if you will, char it is a consuming entity. Whose capital is in Shinar, hence Babylon? We see in verse 3 a woman and a beast. The woman represents evil mankind, and the beast represents the lively organism that propels and/or uses the evil desires of the whore. The color scarlet represents wealth, yes, but also the lust of blood in whatever form, the accomplishing of one's desires at whatever the cost. Let me insert Zechariah 5:5–11 here:

> 5. Then the angel that talked with me went forth, and said unto me, Lift now thine eyes, and see what is this that goeth forth.
> 6. And I said, What is it? And he said, this is an ephah that goeth forth. He said moreover, This is their resemblance through all the earth.
> 7. And, behold, there was lifted up a talent of lead: and this a woman that sitteth in the midst of the ephah?
> 8. And he said, this is wickedness. And he cast it in the midst of the ephah; and he cast the weight of lead upon the mouth thereof
> 9. Then lifted I up mine eyes, and looked, and, behold, there came out two women, and the wind was in their wings; for they had wings like the wings of a stork: and they lifted up the ephah between the earth and the heaven.
> 10. Then said I to the angel that talked with me, Whither do these bear the ephah?
> 11. And he said unto me, To build it an house in the land of Shinar: and it shaff be established, and set there upon her own base.

This beast has seven heads and ten horns; we will cover them later in this chapter. Please see that the foundation, or purpose, of the beast's makeup is to blaspheme the true and living God; in other words, to rebel against the only God—to use the will of evil mankind and the will of evil mankind's religious aspect.

Oh, verse 4! Mankind (yes, it is a religious system, but it is the general makeup of man) is dressed in the colors of wealth and the ornaments of wealth. This city will have such a ferocious appetite for *any* and all pleasure, and consumes in the cup the desires of this chosen life. It takes for granted that the promise

128

of self-gratification is forever true. Looking at the glamour, one could easily lose sight of the great harm to others that has taken place in order to fill that cup. But God does.

In verse 5, we see the realm that Nimrod left behind. Cain's sin was ugly, but Nimrod's life was the benchmark that has been used for an entire religion of self's desires.

Verses 6f show that sin costs someone. It is not always God's people, but it is always God's creation. Please do not scoff at John for admiring. Is there even one who has not sinned, excluding the Lord Jesus Christ, of course? And is not sin very appealing?

What we must do is to realize the subtlety of Satan, sin, and self. A most sobering thought can be seen in 2 Timothy 2:26: *"And that they may recover themselves out of the snare of the devil, who are taken captive by him at his will."* Notice, *"at his will."*

One should see that we are in a battle against evil on the outside and the inside. Satan knows how to get to those things on the inside of each of us that some call "buttons." Yes, we do have desires of one kind or another. We choose whether we will let him have his way, or our self's will, or follow God.

We should let the reality of those words, *"the wine of the wrath of her fornication,"* echo in our minds until their reality sinks its stinking self into our souls. *We should see how our determination to satisfy our selfish desires produces a greater need of self-gratification.* Do we remember God's words in Genesis 6: *"evil continually"*?

> *8. The beast that thou sawest was, and is not; and shall ascend out of the bottomless pit, and go into perdition. And they that dwell on the earth shall wonder, they whose name hath not been written in the book of Life from the foundation of the world, when they behold the beast, how that he was, and is not, and shall come.*
>
> *9. Here is the mind that hath wisdom. The seven heads are seven mountains, on which the woman sitteth:*
>
> *10. And they are seven king;; the five are fallen, the one is, the other is not yet come; and when he cometh, he must continue a little while.*

> *11. And the beast that was, and is not, is himself also an eighth, and is of the seven; and he goeth into perdition.*

We finally have gotten to the part that has stomped on me for so long. In verses 8–11, we find the explanation of the Beast. First, let me set the stage for you.

1. The first beast, or king, is seen in Nimrod. Let's look at Genesis 10:8–10:

> *8. And Cush begat Nimrod. He began to be a mighty one in the earth.*
> *9. He was a mighty hunter before Jehovah. Wherefore it is said, Like Nimrod a mighty hunter before Jehovah.*
> *10. And the beginning of his kingdom was Babel and Erech, and Accad, and Calneh, in the land of Shinar._*

You notice he was mighty before God, and he had a kingdom. From his kingdom all languages sprang, as you will notice in the next chapter of Genesis.

2. Beast number two, a kingdom of world power, is seen in Genesis 41:25, 40, 56f:

> 25. And Joseph said unto Pharaoh, The dream of Pharaoh is one: God hath shewed Pharaoh what he is about to do....
> 40. Thou shalt be over my house, and according unto thy word shall all my people be ruled: only in the throne will I be greater than thou....
> 56. And the famine was over all the face of the earth: and Joseph opened all the storehouses, and sold unto the Egyptians; and the famine waxed sore in the land of Egypt.
> 57. And all countries came into Egypt to Joseph to buy corn, because the famine was so sore in all the earth.

I believe that the second kingdom is this Pharaoh, in particular, his kingdom. It definitely was a kingdom, and the world did come to it for help. I don't have any other proof that this is the second kingdom, except *"and all countries cameinto Egypt"* (Gen. 41:57). But I don't see anywhere else in Scripture a kingdom of world power.

One would mention Solomon, and I would say, that was a "righteous" kingdom. Those who came to Solomon were looking, not coming out of need or being forced. You notice I put righteous in quotation marks. The reason is that even though he was so blessed of God and had been given so much wisdom, he still was affected by sin. He placed in Jerusalem idolatrous altars for his nonbelieving wives to be able to worship their gods. That, to me, folks, is totally ridiculous. However, we have little places in our hearts where we have set up excuses, etc., or just not given to God. People, we are just as foolish as Sodom.

We then come to the four kingdoms in Daniel 2:31ff, which makes six kingdoms.Then he rejuvenated last kingdom of Rome will be the seventh, which is the ten horns of Daniel. These horns will place a single person in charge. He will be very persuasive, will be given power, and three leaders will fall out of power at his taking the position. So that makes seven kingdoms, doesn't it? Now you ask a very pertinent question about the eighth beast: where does this beast come from? Let's go back to our text of verses 8–11.

> 8. *The beast that thou sawest was, and is not; and shall, ascend out of the bottomless pit, and to go into perdition: and they that dwell on the earth shall wonder, whose name were not written in the book of life from the foundation of the world, when they behold the beast, that was, and is not, and yet is.*
>
> 9. *And here is the mind which hath wisdom. The seven heads are seven mountains, on which the woman sitteth:*
>
> 10. *And there are seven kings; five are fallen, the one is, and the other is not yet come; and when hecometh, he must continue a short space.*
>
> 11. *And the beast that was, and is not, then he is the eighth, and is of the seven; and goeth into perdition.*

Remembering chapters 9, 11, and 13, we can see this as the body of the man, the Antichrist, the Beast of the start of the tribulation. This person is killed with a sword, and Lucifer indwells him to keep him alive and to have a vehicle, if you will, in which to lead through. In chapter 9, the devil is loosed from the bottomless pit. In chapter 11, he kills the two witnesses. In chapter 13, he indwells the slain Antichrist.

While you are thinking of verse 10 and the five fallen, remember that John is writing while the old Roman Empire is still in existence.

Now we go to verse 11 and see that Satan is in full control of the religious system and his empire. It is stated that he will go into perdition, into hell, into pain. He will have a demise that is adverse to what he thinks will happen. It is a demise that is shameful and not exalted. Now where is the "I will"? *Thank You, God!*

Now we move on to the next turn of events. Satan, being in full control and yet his empire is suffering from the attacks by God, has to make some decisions about power structure. He has evil mankind in control, but those pesky Jews and those followers of Jesus are a real pain. To win he must eradicate the world of those kinds and concentrate his power in one place. So we go to our next text.

> 12. *And the ten horns which thou sawest are ten kings, which have received no kingdom as yet; but receive power as kings one hour with the beast.*
> 13. *These have one mind, and shall give their power and strength unto the beast.*
> 14. *These shall make war with the Lamb, and the Lamb shall overcome them, for he is Lord of lords, and King of kings: and they that are with him are called, and chosen, and faithful.*

Everybody is getting the big head and wants to be a king; these leaders want their rightful position, a kingship. They set this guy up in power; now they want it back. But it's too late. They have to settle for subservience a little longer. They will have to mount a big battle to win over the forces of righteousness, and then they can have their day.

Satan always promises and promises, and man always loses. Boy, do I think the time of His coming to call us out is close. Praise Him, praise Him. Oh, did you not.ice verse 14? The Lamb shall overcome them. Notice, too, that He fights alongside a select group called *"chosen, and faithful."* It truly is good to know oneself is in this group.

> Calle—All are called to salvation.
> Chosen—The gift of eternal life is so beautiful, and to make rhat choice is sweet.
> Faithful—These haveenduredand have chosen toendure.

We will get to come back for this battle, and all we'll get to say, "I told you He would come back and bust you one."

> *15. And he saith unto me, The waters which thou sawest, where the whore sitteth, are peoples, and multitudes, and nations, and tongues.*
> *16. And the ten horns which thou sawest upon the beast, these shall hate the whore, and shall make her desolate and naked, and shall eat her flesh, and burn her with fire.*
> *17. For God hath put in their hearts to fulfil his will, and to agree, and to give their kingdom unto the beast, until the words of God shall be fulfilled.*

John tells us that the waters are actually the people of the earth, the nations. Grasp that these are controlled, fully dependent people. In verse 16, we see the need to stop supplying the cities' needs and to supply the war effort. The religious factor of these people's lives has become a problem to the kings and must be dealt with. The whore has been stealing the kings' rightful place of exaltation. With hard times on them, they must decide who is going to be in charge. They choose themselves. In verse 17, we see how God uses their self-willed nature to get them to do what He wants done.

When God prophesies something, it will happen. God is working their lives in stages. If they are busy battling their own kingdom, they will nor be hurting His people. Can you imagine the looks on their faces when they get through destroying the great whore? It will be like, "I'm trying to run a race, and I just shot myself in the foot, for *what reason?*" Just a quick note: You do remember the vesture dipped in blood.

> 18. And the woman which thou sawest is the great city, which reigneth over the kings of the earth. [Remember Zechariah 5:5.]

No other city has ruled the kings of the earth as she has. Just a note here:All the beliefs and desires of mankind, which involves self getting its way, are the ways of the great whore. This belief system started with Nimrod.

We saw the forerunner, the foundation if you will, in chapter 2, with the mention of the sect called the Nicolaitanes. Folks, in God's house, there is not a superior position. There is a called position; all His children are equal.

Satan has been so in control, or so he thinks. He has the Western Hemisphere binding together to make a more financially successful whole. The European nations are making a one-country effort, of course. When you look at the possibilities of Africa, the Arab states, and the strengths of the Asian nations all playing for their own concerns, Satan will have his hands full. Need I remind you of what God said in Daniel, that the events will follow *His* schedule. Please remember, the usable land surface has shrunk; hence, mankind is getting close together.

There is one more thought to interject about the world's mind. One could put every human being in the world in their own house measuring forty feet by twenty feet on the dry land surface of Texas and still have room for more. That is seven billion plus.

Now, does it sound like the world is overpopulated? What have the world leaders, or leader, been trying to do? Lucifer's thought is to kill as many humans as he can however he can, thinking it bolsters his position. Hence, we have the different killing ways of the world, which is part of what is in the whore's cup—the harm of many to satisfy a few.

Chapter 18

Chapter 18 is the realization of the last three verses of chapter 16. As chapter 17 was an information chapter, chapter 18 is an events chapter, like Genesis 1 and Genesis 2. God leaves no stone unturned, as it were, or anything to chance, when it comes to the description of how He will settle the score with evil. God was totally serious with His remarks in Revelation 2:22f. You know what? You don't want to mess with God.

> 1. *After these things I saw another angel come down from heaven, having great power; and the earth was lightened with his glory.*
> 2. *And he cried mightily with a strong voice, saying, Babylon the great, is fallen, is fallen, and is become the habitation of devils, and the hold of every foul spirit, and a cage of every unclean and hateful bird.*
> 3. *For all nations have drunk of the wine of the wrath of her fornication, and the kings of the earth have committed fornication with her, and the merchants of the earth are waxed rich through the abundance of her delicacies.*

Think with me for just a moment. Why is this city, this system, this enormous power base referred to as a whore? God is Creator, but more, He wants His creation to have a oneness type relationship with Him. That is why one of His names is El Shaddai—the nourisher, the provider, the husband. He gave Abraham's wife, Sarah, as an example. So, any efforts or thoughts contrary to being consistent with His holiness would be an infraction to our family existence with Him.

A look at chapters 17 and 18 makes one wonder how God is going to get the Beast and the kings to do this to the great whore. The Lord will carry out His own actions, but He will use the enemy to fight itself also. The answer is coming, but you must be patient. Oh, the epitaph of such glamour and power: I offer a thought here.

"Once so great, and with vast power;
The habitation of evil and corruption
Is gone in one hour."

Of all the many things that the great whore will be known for, the best way to describe her would be evil to the max. As Sodom and Gomorrah are readily known for homosexuality, she will be known for lust and depravity. The very sear of self-will and self-gratification will become a cancer of a different kind to the Beast.

4. And I heard another voice from heaven, saying, Come forth, my people, out of her, that ye have no fellowship with her sins, and that ye receive not of her plagues.

Now, God told Elijah that He had seven thousand who had not bowed the knee to Baal (1 Kings 18: 19). I'm sure He will have followers here also. As in Sodom and Gomorrah, God is telling the Christians in the city at that moment in time to get out of the city. Let's not forget Lot.

Daniel 11 tells of many battles and movements of forces and campaigns. I think it is a picture of the battles the Beast will be engaged in also. The Beast of the tribulation is going to be fighting to maintain control of his realm as well as gain control of all the earth.

Now you would think, "Hey, we are talking about Lucifer here, and think of all those demons in his control." But stop and remember: Russia has always been a force of its own, and the Bible does talk about Magog being a threatening force.

We will deal with the battle of Gog and Magog later; it is a separate item, as well as theriver Euphrates being dried up so the kings of the East can come into the Middle East. I know their presence will be in the battle of Armageddon. However, they were not part of the Roman Empire, number one, and they defiantly have a mind of their own.

Satan is attempting to rule the entire world, and mankind is attempting to rule anyrhing and everything. Right or wrong, the city will be destroyed by its so-called friends. I see that it will be a necessity, for the city, as we've seen, consumes enormous amounts of resources. The Beast's forces will make every effort for the gathering of resources and the concentration of efforts. Please remember Revelation 16:13–14:

> *13. And I saw three unclean spirits like frogs come out of the mouth of the dragon, and out of the mouth of the beast, and out of the mouth of the false prophet.*
> *14. For they are the spirits of devils, working miracles, which go forth unto the kings of the earth and of the whole world, to gather them to the battle of that great day of God Almighty.*

And who did someone say was in charge?

> *5. For her sins have reached unto heaven, and God hath remembered her iniquities.*
> *6. Reward unto her even as she rewarded you, and double unto her double according to her works: in the cup which she hath filled fill to her double.*
> *7. How much she hath glorified herself, and lived deliciously, so much torment and sorrow give her: for she saith in her heart, I sit a queen, and am no widow, and shall see no sorrow.*

Bingo! Aha! This is how Satan has grown mankind's lusts. "Let us build a tower," they proclaimed in Genesis 11:4.

> *8. Therefore shall her plagues come in one day, death, and mourning, and famine; and she shall be utterly burned with fire: for strong is the Lord God who judgeth her.*

Boy, mankind is in for it. God's patience is for a reason; His schedule will be followed. In verse 5 and into verse 7, the sins of mankind are so vast, and God has held off judgment for so long, that the sins of the whore have reached unto heaven. As Genesis 15:16 says, *"For the iniquity of the Amorites is not yet full."*

Please compare the queen (the whore) of verse 7 with Eve's words:

1. *Is it not easy to see the mind of Eve in the thoughts of this queen?— "good for food."*
2. *Can we not see the heart of Eve in the queen's words?— "pleasant to the eyes," "wise."*
3. *Is it not easy to see the evil of their self-gratifying actions?— "took," "ate," "gave."*

Eve's goal is summed up in the thoughts of the queen (whore); that is, "I will attain on my own, and I will enjoy it for a long time." But do the words "thou fool" of Christ in Luke 12:1–21 echo as to the reality of verse 8 of our text?

Does anyone remember the Tower of Babel? Instead of man reaching into heaven and saying "Look at what we accomplished, God," their *sins* mounted to that height. Oops! *"And God hath remembered her iniquities."* What an accurate account of the life of sin and the stringent punishment for that sin. You can see in verse 7 a position of power, no losses, no problems: "I am in charge." Ain't life grand? Verse 8, however, shows a different account of life:

a. Plagues
b. Death
c. Mourning
d. Famine
e. Fire

When God brings on the judgment, it's on. Amen!

9. And the kings of the earth, who have committed fornication and lived deliciously with her, shall bewail her, and lament for her, when they shall see the smoke of her burning,

10. Standing a far off for the fear of her torment, saying, Alas, alas, that great city Babylon, that mighty city! for in one hour is thy judgment come.

11. And the merchants of the earth weep and mourn over her, for no man buyeth their merchandise any more.

The world population has been shrinking because of all the killing. But this magnificent city of wealth and the spending of wealth have brought huge profits to merchants and traders alike. But the rulers, including the Beast, have to mount a great offensive. They do not need this city of wealth telling them what to do or getting in the way.

The Beast has corrupted mankind to the extent that his rulers will destroy the whore. That will enable them to gather all of mankind's forces together at the city that has been desired for centuries—Jerusalem.

The merchants will be standing a far off and crying. The world leaders will wonder how they could have been party to the destruction of the very power that brought them wealth. All the while, Satan is in the corner laughing at them. He will have the leaders where he wants them, headed for the big battle. Please, somebody say, "How can this be?"

I'm glad you asked. God said in chapter 17 that His will would be accomplished, and can you figure, but the Lord Jesus Christ is in the middle of it all, orchestrating everything. This is where the vesture that He is wearing in chapter 19 is dipped in blood. Do you remember in chapter 14 that He was sitting on a cloud and He had a sharp sickle?

In the first half of the tribulation, mankind will be jockeying for position and desperate for leadership. Furthermore, they will be suffering from the judgments of God. We see these in chapter 8 and then the beasts of chapter 9.

So stop and think. Just because millions of people have been taken from the earth (in the rapture), does that mean that the only human life in this new kingdom is of the Beast? No. Man will be trying to reestablish the countries and go forward saying, "We told you so. It was the gravitational pull of some rouge planet passing to dose. There will be a very big difference of opinions."

The Holy Spirit will have been taken out; that will mean that the restraining force of righteousness will no longer be here. This means anything goes in each person's mind. Criminal activity will be the thing of the day. As the last few verses of the Book of Judges reads, *"And every man did that which was right in his own eyes."*

In the fuse part of the second half, mankind will have their regional problems, with global problems being more and more devastating. At first mankind will use the earth's resources at will in a devastating way in order to keep up production (latter part of chapter 11). Then the empowered Beast and his forces and his regulations will gain power in drastic proportions.

Then God really gets going on the judgment aspect of this period. So there's little wonder why these leaders pull a stunt like this. There is little wonder why they end up crying about it. They have just destroyed the greatest customer they had left, and it was their own city. Let's take a quick look at these next verses. *Oh, the depravity!*

> *12. The merchandise of gold, and silver, and precious stones, and of pearls, and fine linen, and purple, and silk, and scarlet; and all thyine wood, and all manner vessels of ivory, and manner vessels of most precious wood, and of brass, and iron, and marble;*
> *13. And cinnamon, and odours, and ointments, and frankincense, and wine, and oil, and fine flour, and wheat, and beasts, and sheep; and horses, and chariots, and slaves, and souls of men.*
> *14. And the fruits that thy soul lusteth after are departed from thee, and all things which were dainty and goodly are departed from thee, and thou shalt find them no more at all.*
> *15. The merchants of these things, which were made rich by her, shall stand afar off for the fear of her torment, weeping and wailing,*
> *16. And saying, Alas, ahs that great city, that was clothed in fine linen, and purple, and scarlet, and decked with gold, and precious stones, and pearls!*

> *17. For in one hour so great riches is come to nought. And every shipmaster, and all the company in ships and sailors, and as many as trade by sea, stood afar off,*
>
> *18. And cried when they saw the smoke of her burning, saying, What city is like unto this great city!*
>
> *19. And they cast dust on their heads, and cried, weeping and wailing, saying, Alas, alas that great city, wherein were made rich all that had ships in the sea by reason of her costliness! for in one hour is she made desolate.*

Now, remembering 17:13, Satan has them committed to the coming great battle in the tiny land of Israel. How much of the world's power structure could be left? This is deep into the tribulation; the world has been devastated by God's judgments of chapter 16.

It has been mentioned that maybe the judgments of God are only for the people of the Middle East area. I disagree, and the reason is this: He must get the world to come to His party. Mankind is down to the last few verses of chapter 16. All of mankind will just be trying to survive. Granted, the rulers of the Beast's realm will fare better than most.

Since there will be no unsaved person go into the millennial kingdom of the Lord, all of mankind will be forced to this area from all sections of the globe, to do battle if necessary, to find resomces. Will it be because of oil? I do not know; many things can be manufactured out of oil, including food. Of a certainty, Jerusalem has always been a jewel that the world's leaders have wanted. Furthermore, remember the three spirits that went out of the mouths of the dragon, the Beast, and the False Prophet. Yep, it's time.

But first, let's look at the rest of chapter 18. It is God's way of offering encouragement; this city has a certain doom and will never return, never harm again. The verses speak for themselves. I offer this one thought about these verses: remember when the Lord, hanging on the cross, said, *"It is finished,"* and the statement *"It is done"* in Revelation 16: 17.

142

20. Rejoice over her, thou heaven, and ye holy apostles, and prophets; for God hath avenged you on her.

21. And a mighty angel took up a stone like a great millstone, and cast it into the sea, saying, Thus with violence shaff that great city Babylon, be thrown down, and shaff be found no more at all.

22. And the voice of harpers, and musicians, and of pipers, and trumpeters shall be heard no more at aff in thee; and no craftsman, of whatsoever craft he be, shaff be found any more in thee; and the sound of a millstone shall be heard no more at all in thee;

23. And the light of a candle shall shine no more at all in thee; and the voice of the bridegroom and of the bride shall be heard no more at all in thee: for thy merchants were the great men of the earth; for by thy sorceries were all the nations deceived.

24. And in her was found the blood of prophets, and of saints, and of all that were slain upon the earth.

As we visualize the great waves crashing in on top of the sinking great millstone, we get a sneak preview of what total annihilation is all about. This destruction will be sudden. The Beast and his ten kings thought they did a good thing, a necessary thing. All the while, they were following God's lead and had God's help. When God says He will get you, He will. Looking at 6:15f and 16:19ff, along with 17:16, one can see they are fulfilled in chapter 18. Those fortunate enough to be outside the city seeing the carnage, the vast sudden destruction, can only hide and pray to be destroyed quickly. *They will refuse to repent.*

Satan and the ten kings will have accomplished their job in gathering the world to one battle. More importantly, God will have accomplished His will.

Some think that this last mention of the city Babylon is the Babylon of the Old Testament. It is not. Scripture is still referring to the whore of chapter 17. Notice please, *"For by thy sorceries were all the nations deceived."*

Chapter 19

The events of chapter 19 must follow Deuteronomy 24:5: *"When a man hath taken a new wife, he shall not go out to war, neither shall he be charged with any business: but he shall be free at home one year, and shall cheer up his wife which he hath taken."* The events are as follows:

a. He has a duty to the wife of one year. This is to secure the wife in the family and to secure her future by hopefully giving her a child. As we have and will see, all of heaven is ours; therefore, we are secure already. Glorified and earthly mankind will get to enjoy the grandeur of the presence of the Lord for a thousand years, not just one.

b. Any warring will have to have been taken care of before the wedding, which the Lord is about to handle. I know the battle of Armageddon will happen after the marriage supper, but the Bridegroom only has to speak to win.

c. Family life for newlyweds is hard enough without the pressures of business; therefore, there will be no affairs of state, which 20:1–6 takes care of. These were alluded to in the last four verses of chapter 2.

Now, folks, I know the Lord is always in control, but the verse in Deuteronomy is a picture of what is about to happen. Remember, Jesus is the Word of God and the God of His Word. The Lord will marry; He and His bride will take a ride and enter a new kingdom. *Wow, what a wedding gift!* A river of life will flow, and a kingdom will flourish.

1. And after these things I heard a great voice of much people in heaven, saying, Alleluia; Salvation, and glory, and honour, and power, unto the Lord our God:

2. For true and righteous are his judgments: for he hath judged the great whore, which did corrupt the earth with her fornication, and hath avenged the Mood of his servants at her hand.

3. And again they said, Alleluia. And her smoke rose up for ever and ever.

4. And the four and twenty elders and the four beasts fell down and worshipped God that sat on the throne, saying, Amen; Alleluia.

5. And a voice came out of the throne, saying, Praise our God, all ye his servants, and ye that fear him, both small and great.

6. And I heard as it were the voice of a great multitude, and as the voice of many waters, and as the voice of mighty thunderings, saying, Alleluia: for the Lord God omnipotent reigneth.

The clean up of the kingdom has started. There are several things to notice in these verses:

1. The saints of the ages will be shouting out in victory over the great whore. Righteous mankind has suffered at the hand of the emissaries of this self-religious system. As we've seen, it started with Eve and Adam. We will have watched the different vials being poured out, and we will have shouted out in victory, yes. However, when this whore goes under, never to return, it is the beginning of the end of evil. Oh, what a happy day, as is expressed in these first three verses.

2. Verse 4 expresses the joy of the elders. But why are the four beasts mentioned? It is a throne scene; remember, this is the throne of righteousness. We are taken back

145

to chapter 4, and the very purpose of this throne and of this book: the end of sin and the establishing of the kingdom.

3. In verse 5, is this the Lord Jesus Christ? More than likely it is. The reason why is the same: the Lord Jesus Christ was the humble Adam that Adam was not. He was given all power and has brought about the end of the whore. Yes, but much more, He has initiated the setting up of righteousness. The righteous humble Adam is getting ready for a reign of righteousness.

4. All of heaven then responds to the Lord with a great alleluia in verse 6.

7. Let us be glad and rejoice, and give honour to him: for the marriage of the Lamb is come, and his wife hath made herself ready.

8. And to her was granted that she should be arrayed in fine linen, clean and white: for the fine linen is the righteousness of saints.

9. And he saith unto me, Write, Blessed are they which are called unto the marriage supper of the Lamb. And he saith unto me, These are the true sayings of God

The Lord left His church behind to do His will of spreading the gospel. All of the activities of mankind to follow the will of God have come to this moment in these verses. Oh, the joy of these verses! To this point, all the demands of righteousness have been met. It is time for the arrival of the King on His estate. Tears well up in my eyes at the thought of this time. Glory, glory, glory! We *are* going home to be with Him there. We will come back and enjoy His victory here.

These three verses express so much beauty and pomp, but not a prideful pomp. Beautiful white linen will be ours. All the saints through the ages will be standing in awe of the scene that is taking place. All the angels will attend in reverence. Oh, do you remember we have already gotten our rewards, and how

146

that was a scene of extreme splendor? But here, my friends, we will be in the marriage of the Lamb. What a beautiful scene. I do look forward to it.

Just like the ruler that the Lord mentions in Luke 19:1–27 who goes away to take a kingdom, the Lord has done what He needed here on earth. His subjects are to abide and to gain for the Lord. He must deal with the unruly servants who would not follow Him.

As we have seen in our text, the glorified humans are making ready for the marriage of the Lamb. The Lord is about to set up His earthly kingdom; however, for His kingdom to be peaceful, He must destroy the discontented citizens first, which is, of course, the battle of Armageddon. He will set up His governmental rule in the city of Jerusalem. The marriage supper itself will take place next.

The marriage will be a scene of the Ruler establishing His kingdom. There will be food and fellowship, and peace. The humans who knew Jesus Christ as their Savior and lived to the battle of Armageddon will go into the thousand-year reign of Christ. The 144,000 are among these.

Think with me for a minute. The needs of the 144,000 will have been met, but for the rest, can you imagine going from scratching for food and decent water co a banquet like this? Can you imagine going from rags to riches? Oh, the tears come gushing forth! No more starving, no more being destitute of the simple things of life. No more being hunted to death. No more deceit. No more homelessness, hiding anywhere you can to keep out of sight and always looking over your shoulder. No more wondering if you own family will turn you in for a reward.

There will be no need of a doctor and not having one as you watch your injuries get infected. No, instead, there will be health, food, water, provisions of all kinds, and *peace.*

Oh, what a happy day that will be, for them to go from cringing in the darkness of their hiding places hoping for the daylight—the very same thing they had done in the day, hoping they could make it through the day, to be hidden by the dark. Can you even begin to imagine the relief? Oh, God!

His commanders (us) will have their jobs to do to monitor mankind. Of course, the Lord will always know what is going on; however, the kingdom life will be a life of righteousness. Sin will be dealt with speedily and harshly; remember the last few verses of chapter 2.

> 10. *And I fell at his feet to worship him. And he said unto me, See thou do it not: I am thy fellowservant, and of thy brethren that have the testimony of Jesus: worship God: for the testimony of Jesus is the spirit of prophecy.*

Could John have become so overwhelmed with the grandeur that he tried to worship the angel? How could he, realizing he was not the Lord? Well, anyway, it happened. The important thing is to realize this emotion can happen and must be guarded against. Keep telling the story of the coming Savior. God's Word is finished; there are no more prophecies to be given. But the spirit of prophecy is to tell others about Jesus Christ. We must put Jesus Christ first and keep our eyes on Him. We must keep a sober attitude about what is happening around us. John was overwhelmed at what he was experiencing; we *must* keep our eyes on Jesus.

> 11. *And I saw heaven opened, and behold a white horse; and he that sat upon him was called Faithful and True, and in righteousness he doth judge and make war.*
> 12. *His eyes were as a flame of fire, and on his head were many crowns; and he had a name written, that no man knew, but he himself.*
> 13. *And he was clothed with a vesture dipped in blood· and his name is called The Word of God.*
> 14. *And the armies which were in heaven followed him upon white horses, clothed in fine Linen, white and clean.*
> 15. *And out of his mouth goeth a sharp sword, that with it he should smite the nations: and he shall rule them with a rod*

of iron: and he treadeth the winepress of the fierceness and
wrath of Almighty God
16. And he hath on his vesture and on his thigh a name written,
KING OF KINGS, AND LORD OF LORDS.

You know, as we look at the Lord Jesus Christ here in this scene, something has always puzzled me about the name that no one knew. Of course, we saw this in the second chapter also. But, you see, we are now to the events of chapter 22, so the beauty of these names can't be seen until all evil is gone.

We see the vesture dipped in blood. This conquering King is a battler, like Abraham. Remember that chapter 14, where the Lord is sitting on a cloud, pictures His actions taken against the whore, given in chapters 16–18. All of this He Himself prophesied in 2:18–23.

In verse 13, we see this one (the name) that no one could understand but He Himself. In Genesis, God created and said, *"But of the tree of the knowledge of good and evil thou shalt not eat of it: for in the day that thou eatest thereof thou shalt surely die."* Christ will be fulfilling that scripture—the Word of God. God is truly patient. Adam and Eve died spiritually when they ate of the fruit; now evil mankind will be dying physically for sin. You see, God has a special relationship one-on-one with each of us. We individually will know how God relates to us, for He will call us by our names, just as we parents call our children by special names. Ain't God neat?

Verse 14 shows His armies will be dressed in beautiful white clothes. Key point, they will stay that way.

Verses 15f show how the Lord does battle. He only has to speak and His word is done. Remember the two witnesses of chapter 11; they could protect themselves in the same way. They died at the time appointed for them; their ministry was complete. To complete His earthly ministry, Jesus had to die, but He arose. The title of KING OF KINGS AND LORD OF LORDS belongs only to Him. No one can challenge His authority or His power. Those who do so die by the words that He speaks.

17. And I saw an angel standing in the sun; and he cried with a loud voice, saying to all the fowls that fly in the midst of heaven, Come and gather yourselves together unto the supper of the great God;

18. That ye may eat the flesh of kings, and the flesh of captains, and the flesh of mighty men, and the flesh of horses, and of them that sit on them, and the flesh of all men, both free and bond, both small and great.

The gathering of the nations to do battle is a most impressive thing to contemplate. To get the flesh off the ground, the Lord will call the birds of prey to gather also. Satan has put everything in order for a victory only he could imagine. He will also be directing the activity of the three demons out of the mouths of the evil trinity. On the one hand, the Lord has driven mankind to the valley of Megiddo in the plain of Jezreel. On the other, Satan has seduced and manipulated them to this spot. Are you ready?

19. And I saw the beast, and the kings of the earth, and their armies, gathered together to make war against him that sat on the horse, and against his army.

Now the forces of evil will be quite impressive. Seasoned warriors and desperate people will be led by arrogance. Have you ever pulled the hopper legs off a grasshopper, messed up the mound of a red-ant bed, and then dropped the grasshopper in? There is no mercy. When the battle is engaged, there will be no mercy, for none is deserved. Mercy was not accepted when offered. Mercy was not extended to His children. Mercy cannot be extended now; evil must be squashed.

One could goon to the next verse and it might be okay. Please consider this: a valley five miles wide and twenty-five miles long will be filled with valiant, as well as desperate and duped, people. Some have lived a "good" flamboyant life, living in excess. Others have done without and have great needs. They have armor and sophisticated weapons and highly trained personnel. Life's dreams of an evil empire that not even He could touch looms in the heads of millions. Whatever you folks can think of about the thoughts of these people that could have them in this very spot will be the lure to get them in the valley. Think of the desperation in these lives. Think of the anxiety of these people.

Then this massive force shows up on horses, with no real weapons that one can see. Where you were possibly scared at first as your forces gathered, now your enemy shows up, and not really ready for battle. This must be a joke.

Now do you understand what Hebrews 4 is telling you? We rest here. We ride and watch then. Ain't it great to be on the winning team? *Now* and *then.*

> 20. *And the beast was taken, and with him the false prophet that wrought miracles before him, with which he deceived them that had received the mark of the beast, and them that worshipped his image. These both were cast alive into a lake of fire burning with brimstone.*
> 21. *And the remnant were slain with the sword of him that sat upon the horse, which sword proceeded out of his mouth: and all the fowls were filled with their flesh.*

What a scene of death! Does one think that chicken Lucifer made a quick getaway? The indwelled Beast is taken as well as the False Prophet, and they are cast alive into the lake of fire. No, Lucifer is captured and put into the bottomless pit in the next chapter.

Let me add some thoughts here:

> We know the lake of fire is not on the earth, because the earth in the thousand-year reign of Christ is going to be a beautiful place. It will be similar to the Garden of Eden. The reason is this: mankind has had its opportunity of self-rule without Satan and failed. Now they will have a world of total righteousness and will still have unsaved humans at the end. Not one human will beable to point

151

a finger at God with some made-up excuse that it was God's fault that they failed to know Him.

We know the Beast had been slain and indwelled at the midway point of the tribulation. Now he is cast into the lake of fire, alive. God is going to bring his soul and spirit back to his eternal body so he can burn forever. Will the folks in the valley be able to run? Not fast enough. Get 'em, God!

One should give some thought here to the gatherings God has done in the past. In Egypt, God brought millions of frogs, flies, locusts, and lice. He sent tons of manna and quail to the children of Israel while they were in the wilderness. God's gathering of the birds of prey to eat and to suck up the blood will be an awesome grandstand for these participants to see. If they believe in bad omens, and these folks will, there is going to be some scared folks. But it will be too late; their death will be sudden. *There will be no survivors.*

The one called the Word of God will fulfill the words of God.

Chapter 20

> *1. And I saw an angel come down from heaven, having the key of the bottomless pit and a great chain in his hand*
>
> *2. And he laid hold on the dragon, that old serpent, which is the Devil, and Satan, and bound him a thousand years,*
>
> *3. And cast him into the bottomless pit, and shut him up, and set a seal upon him,that he should deceive the nations no more, till the thousand years should be fulfilled: and after that he must be loosed a little season.*

So, ol'-mad-as-a-hornet Lucifer possibly sees that same angel coming down with a chain, and is chained and put back into his old cage. I can just see his arms and feet flaying around like a spoiled brat. Go get him, God! It sure is nice to know what is going to happen before it happens. And just think—he knows this too but is too set on himself and committed to his way to accept it. Maybe that is oneof the reasons why God hates stubbornness; His creation is supposed to be usable.

You did notice that it didn't take millions of archangels. It took only one angel. Now, he did have a great chain. But chis varmint had to obey the command of God. Does this not tell us *who* is in charge? Does this not humble us and at the same time reassure us about our God?

> *4. And I saw thrones, and they sat upon them, and judgment was given unto them: and I saw the souls of them that were beheaded for the witness of Jesus, and for the word of God, and which had not worshipped the beast, neither*

his image, neither had received his mark upon their foreheads, or in their hands; and they lived and reigned with Christ a thousand years.

5. But the rest of the dead lived not again until the thousand years were finished. This is the first resurrection.

6. Blessed and holy is he that hath part in the first resurrection: on such the second death hath no power, but they shall be priests of God and of Christ, and shall reign with him a thousand years.

Ah, God never forgets. Do you remember Revelation 6:9–11?

9. And when he had opened the fifth seal, I saw under the altar the souls of them that were slain for the word of God, and for the testimony which they held:

10. And they cried with aloud voice, saying, How long, O Lord, holy and true, dost thou not judge and avenge our blood on them that dwell on the earth?

11. And white robes were given unto every one of them; and it was said unto them, that they should rest yet for a little season, until their fellow servants also and their brethren, that should be killed as they were, should be fulfilled.

God is going to set up so many thrones in the kingdom of the thousand-year reign. The four verses of our text, coupled with the ones of chapter 6, show the resurrected tribulation saints reigning with us. God does not overlook or forget His children; remember our prayers of chapter 8. My friends, oftentimes we serve, and it seems our service has no recognition. Be encouraged by these verses and the knowledge that God does not forget; *everything* is marked down. Boy, how I wish I could erase a few things (okay, several things) on my ledger.

Now, while we get ready for the battle of Gog and Magog, let's consider some things about the thousand-year reign of Christ on this earth.

When the tribulation ended, were there any unsaved who went into the thousand-year reign? No. The forces of good and evil were set, and when Jesus opened His mouth to proclaim destruction on evil, all unsaved died. This is His kingdom He is setting up, and no unclean thing will enter into it. How about an amen here!

When the saved individuals who survived the tribulation enter the kingdom, what will be their purpose? That, my friend, is a very good question. If Adam had chosen obedience and eaten of the Tree of Life, what would have been the outcome? Another good question. Would there have been a thousand-year reign? You folks are sure on a roll. The last two questions we can only speculate about. Let's first examine the purpose of life in the thousand-year reign.

God will be glorified. The Old Testament tells of life being healthy and extended. The ground will yield fruit in wholesomeness and beauty. I do rather doubt that commerce will be like we see it today. It will not be hard to get food because the ground will bring forth in abundance. So life will revert back to a simple, garden-type way of life. Life today means pollution and sinful pleasure, things that will not be tolerated.

Sin will be judged in a rod-of-iron fashion. The reason is that God will not permit His kingdom on this earth to be soiled by sin. Mankind will have an opportunity to live in a righteous, well-provided- for world. No more saying "the devil made me do it." Remember, he's locked away. When a person brings a matter of judgment before one of the many thrones, swift judgment will be handed out and fulfilled.

Of course, God knows all things. Mankind was created in innocence and with perfect knowledge of his world; he named the animals, etc. He had to choose to obey or to rebel. We know the outcome. If man had chosen the Tree of Life, Satan and his angels probably would have been judged and put into the lake of fire at that time.

When you look at Genesis 1, you would think that mankind could have reproduced before the fall. It would appear that it would have been possible; however, God, knowing all things, knew that was not going to be. If Adam and Eve didn't sin but had children, would there have been an opportunity to sin later? Again, this would appear a possibility, but really it just doesn't serve much use to speculate about it.

Man was created perfect and was created with a will. Using that will, he chose wrongly.

This is best seen in Revelation 9:20–21:

> *20. The rest of the men which were not killed by these plagues yet repented not of the works of their hands, that they should not worship devils, and idols of gold, and silver, and brass, and stone, and of wood: which neither can see, nor hear, nor walk:*
>
> *21. Neither repented they of their murders, nor of their sorceries, nor of their fornication, nor of their thefts.*

If Adam had eaten of the Tree of Life, everything would have been different. It would have shown a commitment to obedience, a decision similar to the decision of the good angels.

God is not going to come up with a hit-and-miss plan. Evil had to be judged. God will be honored by His creation. So, would there have been a thousand-year reign? I doubt that. Now on to more important matters.

> *7. And when the thousand years are expired, Satan shall be loosed out of his prison,*
>
> *8. And shall go out to deceive the nations which are in the four quarters of the earth, Gog, and Magog, to gather them together to battle: the number of whom is as the sand of the sea.*
>
> *9. And they went upon the breadth of the earth, and compassed the camp of the saints about, and the beloved city: and fire came down from God out of heaven, and devoured them.*

Mankind's thoughts, being evil continually, are going to be given the chance to be front stage. After a thousand years of plenty, and a life of health and swift justice, man is still going to choose evil. God just wanted to prove His point. Lucifer is given the chance to offer corruption to mankind. As we see in verse 8, they are ready to oblige; it will be a vast multitude.

Will Satan have his angels to help in the seduction? It does not say, but I personally think they will already be in the lake of fire with the Beast and the False Prophet. They are not mentioned in verse 10. Anyway, the unbelieving nature of mankind proves for all to see that he is evil and deserves judgment. Mankind will not be able to say no one told them of the importance of following God. I believe that all of unbelieving mankind will be killed at this time. There will be no unbeliever alive to go into the white throne judgment.

In verse 9, God brings about the final blow to evil. Could He have done this before? Yes. God, however, will follow His righteousness and His plan because He is always right.

10. And the devil that deceived them was cast into the lake of fire and brimstone, where the beast and the false prophet are, and shall be tormented day and night for ever and ever.

What a happy day that will be when verses 9f takes place. It is so good to think of this occasion, but the occasion will take care of itself. We are still here on this side of the tribulation, which means we still have a job to do. There is a very sobering occasion coming. There will be no more loosing of Lucifer; he will be there forever. There will be no more temptation, no more feasting on the sadness of mankind. Mr. Ugly ain't coming back anymore. *Amen, amen!*

11. And I saw a great white throne, and him that sat on it, from whose face the earth and the heaven fled away; and there was found no place for them.
12. And I saw the dead, small and great, stand before God; and the books were opened: and another book

157

was opened, which is the book of life:and the dead were judged out of those things which were written in the books, according to their works.

13. And the sea gave up the dead which were in it; and death and hell delivered up the dead which were in them:and they were judged every man according to their works.

14. And death and hell were cast into the lake of fire. This is the second death.

15. And whosoever was not found written in the book of life was cast into the lake of fire.

I must take some time to tell you of the books.

The "Book of Life of the Lamb," the "Lamb's Book of Life," and the "Book of Life" are the same book. Revelation 13:8 reads, *"And all that dwell upon the earth shall worship him, whose names are not written in the book of life of the Lamb slain from the foundation of the world";* and Revelation 3:5 says, *"He that overcometh, the same shall be clothed in white raiment; and I will not blot his name out of the book of life, but I will confess his name before my Father, and before his angels."* These verses, as well as other verses, show that the Creator knew the following:

    a. He knew everyone who would be conceived.

    b. He knew the name that they should have.

    c. It is given here that the Lord knew that He would die for His creation. The Lord being the manager, and knowing that not all of His creation would accept Him, had to have a way of managing life, hence the Lamb's Book of Life.

    2. Next come the books of our lives: *"And the dead were judged out of those things which were written in the books, according to their works."* Do not think that there will be degrees of intensity in the lake of fire. It will be a lake, and

it will be on fire. One would be tempted to think, "How cruel." Please remember the one who said "do not eat" is the same one who died on the cross.

No one who belongs in it will be able to escape this judgment. Death, hell, the sea-wherever an unsaved person is, they will be found and brought to this judgment. When a person dies and has not accepted Jesus Christ as their Savior, their name is blotted out of the Lamb's Book of Life.

Yes, Romans 2:14f does tell of a humility that though they have not heard of Christ, yet they are in humble peace with their creator because they are humble before Him. When a person reaches the moment of mentally leaving childhood and in maturity realizes right from wrong, in particular, that they are responsible to someone, they become accountable. Let us continue.

The throne of righteousness has just ended and now is the white throne judgment. Now somebody tell me what white represents. That's right, righteousness. That should mean that anyone who is not righteous will have a problem.

God has faced many sad times in each of our lives. He has one last sad thing to do: read the books and pronounce the judgment. Then He has to watch unsaved mankind be thrown into the lake of fire. We are to be by His side; therefore, we will be watching all of the events.

This will be the most somber time of our lives as we watch people we know and others as their lives are read and their judgment set. Will there be tears, crying, and halting from these folks, or will it be like cattle to the slaughter? It really doesn't say here, but one should know there will be no power to resist in these folks. There will only be one power, and that is God. God states rather matter-of-factly, *"And whosoever was not found written in the book of life was cast into the lake of fire."*

There will be no time for hesitation or good-byes. We will stand and watch and understand. I believe sadness will be great, but righteousness will be done. As these scriptures state, there will be no place for the lost dead to hide; they will be found and receive their judgment. Are we Philadelphian or Laodicean? That is the choice we have to make. Will we be lackadaisical and add to the sadness of God and ourselves, or will we add stars to our crowns?

Oh, friends, consider the seriousness of this last paragraph.

Chapter 21

Let's start this chapter by reading Psalm 19:1–4:

1. The heavens declare the glory of God; and the firmament sheweth his handywork.

2. Day unto day uttereth speech, and night unto night sheweth knowledge.

3. There is no speech nor language, where their voice is not heard.

4. Their line is gone out through all the earth, and their words to the end of the world. In them hath he set a tabernacle for the sun.

I believe that the salvation story is seen in the stars. God does nothing just for the sake of it. I can't see Him opening His imagination of making stars and just throwing a bunch out there: "Yeah, that ought to do it: a little over here and a little more over there. Yep, all finished." No, as the above verses proclaim, the stars declare the glory of God.

Verse 2 says they have speech and show knowledge. Not only does God have something to say in the stars, but He also uses them to show knowledge, and in every language. Every language has something to say about the stars. What a way to make a statement that every human being has looked at and wondered about and been in awe of.

Folks, I'm a fundamentalist, independent Baptist. That means I believe in the fundamental truths of the Bible as the guideline to life and religious belief. It also means that no church has power over another church. I follow the Baptist distinctives, methods, if you will. I said that to say this: in the book *The Real Meaning of the Zodiac* by Dr. D. James Kennedy, I found it very informative about the constellations.

I know I told you that I would not use any other person's books or messages to write this book. I'm not quoting from it, just letting you know of a resource about the stars. (I must have lent my copy of his book to someone because I haven't seen it since 1997.) However, the stars did not just get there, and his book is of great help about the stars. It, like this book, is just that, a book; it is not Scripture, and neither is this book that I am writing. I'm just trying to answer some nagging questions in my own feeble way. Since God is not foolish, and Psalm 19 is Holy Scripture, God has something to say in all of His creation.

Now just think for a minute. Speech means an ability to communicate. Knowledge means information of value. Just where did the languages start, in their diversity? Also, where did the wise men come from? Did they only have some knowledge of a Savior by way of the Jews in the captivity of Daniel's time?

> Author's Note: I think the wise men had the wisdom of Daniel's erra and place, but I think they came from another place-but that will be discussed in another book.

Yes, but their words show that they were using information from the stars. Did they combine all of their acquired knowledge? Yes. Now, folks, I'm not talking about the use of fortune-tellers; I'm talking about the use of the meaning of the constellations. Had they (the Magi) been exposed to Isaiah 7:14? Yes, but they still followed the stars and the timing of the stars and the angel that God sent before them in the form of a star.

I believe the stars declare the salvation story. In the Book of Revelation, we've reached the end of sin. Therefore, the earth's purpose has been accomplished. We see that the first verse of chapter 21 is a major change:

> *1. And I saw a new heaven and a new earth: for the first heaven and the first earth were passed away; and there was no more sea.*

We see that it is a time for change. God must change our world from the world of the opportunity of sin to the new kingdom of righteousness. As 2 Peter 3:10–14 says:

> *10. But the day of the Lord will come as a thief in the night; in the which the heavens shall pass away with a great noise, and the elements shall melt with fervent heat, the earth also and the works that are therein shall be burned up.*
>
> *11. Seeing then that all these things shall be dissolved, what manner of persons ought ye to be in all holy conversation and godliness,*
>
> *12. Looking for and hasting unto the coming of the day of God, wherein the heavens being on fire shall be dissolved, and the elements shall melt with fervent heat?*
>
> *13. Nevertheless we, according to his promise, look for new heavens and a new earth, wherein dwelleth righteousness.*
>
> *14. Wherefore, beloved, seeing that ye look for such things, be diligent that ye may be found of him in peace, without spot, and blameless.*

Did I say earlier that God is in control? Well, we all know that God is in control. Yes, but sometimes we lose sight of it. From the very moment that Lucifer thought "I will," even to this first verse, God has, like always, been in control.

So why does He have co get rid of all the beautiful sights that mankind is just now peeping into with his sophisticated telescopes? We have been able to see beauties and wonders that have never been imagined.

God put the stars and all that stuff up there for a reason. The salvation story will not be needed at the time of verse 1. He promised a new heaven and a new earth, and now He provides it. No reproduction of species will be taking place. No sin will be there.

163

That brings up a thought: "Yeah, but what if someone decides to say 'I will'?" The new kingdom is a righteous kingdom, a glorified kingdom. If someone decides to be a Lucifer, there will be quick judgment, and the lake of fire awaits. But you must realize that the ones in this kingdom are "called," have been saved. Then you say, "What about the ones who died before the age of accountability and are in heaven because of God's grace?" I do not think that they will see a need or desire to sin. Granted, I don't know everything, and that's easy to see, but one must realize that the kingdom will be set up *in* righteousness.

The Book of Hebrews says that Christ will never suffer again at the hands of man. He suffered, because of sin, once for all. John 14:2 says, *"In my Father's house are many mansions: if it were not so, I would have told you."* We should take the truthfulness of God expressed in John and put in the statement of Hebrews 9:28: *"So Christ was once offered to bear the sins of many; and unto them that look for him shall he appear the second time without sin unto salvation."* We can see that God is not going to travel this road again. Notice in this verse it says *"without sin."* It means in righteousness. We should realize, too, that where He is, sin will not be allowed. I believe full well that the battle of Gog and Magog will be the last opportunity for sin.

This new heaven and new earth are clean and pure. le is the presentation of the holy kingdom to the Father. Oh, with tears in my eyes at such agony that has gone on, but think of it: the kingdom will be presented to the Father. *Amen and amen!*

> *2. And I John saw the holy city, new Jerusalem, coming down from God out of heaven, prepared as a bride adorned for her husband.*

Our eternal abode is now on the scene. There are no more battles and no more trials to go through. It will be beautiful. Look at verses 3—8:

> *3. And I heard a great voice out of heaven saying, Behold, the tabernacle of God is with men, and he will dwell with*

them, and they shall be his people, and God himself shall be with them, and be their God.

4. And God shall wipe away all tears from their eyes; and there shall be no more death, neither sorrow, nor crying, neither shall there be any more pain: for the former things are passed away.

5. And he that sat upon the throne said, Behold, I make all things new. And he said unto me, Write: for these words are true and faithful.

6. And he said unto me, It is done. I am Alpha and Omega, the beginning and the end. I will give unto him that is a thirst of the fountain of the water of life freely.

7. He that overcometh shall inherit all things; and I will be his God, and he shall be my son.

8. But the fearful, and unbelieving, and abominable, and murderers, and whoremongers, and sorcerers, and idolaters, and all liars, shall have their part in the lake which burneth with fire and brimstone: which is the second death.

This time when God proclaims a finish, *"It is done"* in verse 6 (glory!), the kingdom of God is His to enjoy and for us to enjoy. All sorrow is gone. All sin is gone. Happy life with God on a moment- by-moment basis is now our reality. Everything is pure and holy, and fellowship is sweet and forever. Oh, precious Lord! If that doesn't bring tears of joy to your eyes, your tear glands are broken.

Verses 3f tell of our position and God's desire toward us. That will be such an awesome scene, like a little child all snuggled up in their father's arms. Verses 5–8 are an invitation to see and believe and live, or not. They also tell what a person will get as they make up their mind about God.

On the one hand, we see God's attention and love and provisions, no tears, no death, no sorrow, no crying, and no pain. All of life as we know it here will be done away with. These are beautiful thoughts.

On the other hand, those who are fearful, unbelieving, abominable, murderers, whoremongers, sorcerers, idolaters, or liars have been judged to a death by an eternal fire. Gee, is this such a hard choice? I wonder! Do we live like we have hope? More about heaven's scene later.

> *9. And there came unto me one of theseven angels which had the seven vials full of the seven fast plagues, and talked with me, saying, Comehither, I will shew thee the bride, the Lamb's wife.*

Do you see that the bride is one? There will be no governmental structure in the bride. We will be holy because of what He did for us and by our accepting the gift of salvation. We are presented here as one, and not many. The tears have been wiped away, and home is prepared for occupancy. Oh boy! While the Lord hung on the cross and cried, *"It is finished,"* He could look down through time and see this scene. We, too, can use His faith and see this scene. My friends, heaven *is* waiting for us. Do tears of joy leap to your eyes? They do to mine.

> *10. And he carried me away in the spirit to a great and high mountain, and shewed me that great city, the holy Jerusalem, descending out of heaven from God,*
>
> *11. Having the glory of God: and her light was like unto a stone most precious, even like a jasper stone, clear as crystal;*
>
> *12. And had a wall great and high, and had twelve gates, and at the gates twelve angels, and names written thereon, which are the names of the twelve tribes of the children of Israel·*
>
> *13. On the east three gates; on the north three gates; on the south three gates; and on the west three gates.*
>
> *14. And the wall of the city had twelve foundations, and in them the names of the twelve apostles of the Lamb.*
>
> *15. And he that talked with me had a golden reed to measure the city, and the gates thereof, and the wall thereof.*

16. And the city lieth foursquare, and the length is as large as the breadth: and he measured the city with the reed, twelve thousand furlongs. Thel ength and the breadt hand the height of it are equal.

17. And he measured the wall thereof, an hundred and forty and four cubits, according to the measure of a man, that is, of the angel.

18. And the building of the wall of it was of jasper: and the city was puregold, like unto clear glass.

19. And the foundations of the wall of the city were garnished with all manner of precious stones. The first foundation was jasper; the second, sapphire; the third, a chalcedony; the fourth, an emerald;

20. The fifth, sardonyx; the sixth, sardius; the seventh, chrysolite; the eighth, beryl; the ninth, a topaz; the tenth, a chrysoprasus; the eleventh, a jacinth; the twelfth, an amethyst.

21. And the twelve gates were twelve pearls: every several gate was of one pearl: and the street of the city was pure gold, as it were transparent glass.

Some are trying to teach that if we are not quite good enough, we will be attending the gates. This is a totally false teaching. You did notice there was one angel at each gate. Folks, you are either in Christ and He is sufficient, or you are not in Christ.

Let's take a quick look here. The twelve gates mean the accessibility of heaven is ample. The twelve tribes mean we all have a part to do, and God does not overlook anyone or anyone's efforts. They could not all be of the tribe of Judah, the tribe of the King. All the family members of God's house are important. God started a theme and stayed with it. He is not a simple minded person; just look at the vastness of creation.

The wall itself will have a green color to it, more than likely. Jasper, while dear, can have colors, with green being predominant. We should remember the glow of the throne in chapter 4.

Looking at the twelve foundations, we see the following:

a. We see the steadfastness of God's efforts. He uses many humans in all of life, but everything is still founded on Him.

b. He uses the beauty of His creation to show His splendor. Can you imagine the brilliant glow of the city?

Considering this scene and these two paragraphs, look at Hebrews 11:8–10:

8. By faith Abraham, when he was called to go out into a place which he should after receive for an inheritance, obeyed; and he went out, not knowing whither he went.

9. By faith he sojourned in the land of promise, as in a strange country, dwelling in tabernacles with Isaac and Jacob, the heirs with him of the same promise:

10. For he looked for a city which hath foundations, whose builder and maker is God.

These three verses sum up a life of many extenuating circumstances, but he still stood for God. Every child of God has a faraway look of longing for God, and one day our eyes shall behold Him.

Consider, please, that the size of the city is just over 1,322 miles square. If you draw a square along the longitude and the latitude lines from the Canadian border to San Antonio, Texas, and from San Francisco to Oklahoma City, you would pretty well have the equivalent square. You can sure have a lot of mansions in a thing like that.

The angels do not have a home. I guess they don't need one, yet God provides for us a mansion. I think it was Dr. Clarence Larkin who suggested that the city would be equal in length and width and would be high in the middle, kind of like a pyramid. I do nor know if that's it or if it will be cube-like. It just won't matter when we get there. By the way, Dr. Larkin's book *The Spirit World* is an excellent book.

No matter what, just keep looking for the city; it is an anchor for the soul. You see, folks, as we look at what God has brought us through and have our mind's eye on His city, the road we are asked to travel just doesn't seem as hard. *Amen.*

> *22. And I saw no temple therein: for the Lord God Almighty and the Lamb are the temple of it.*
>
> *23. And the city had no need of the sun, neither of the moon, to shine in it: for the glory of God did lighten it, and the Lamb is the light thereof.*

You talk about good times-this is a good-time city! The unbelievable light of the Godhead will make the city of gemstones a most beautiful sight. Considering that, and the light coming off the golden streets, there will not be a shadow in the city. Pretty neat, huh?

These verses mention the Lord God Almighty and the Lamb. Now, in the throne of chapter 4, there was one on the throne, and seven lamps were mentioned, which represented the Holy Spirit. Please remember that throne did not include by name the Father, but He is there in the center. It is the throne of righteousness, which is to bring about a righteous kingdom to the Father. This a scene of the Godhead dealing with their creation. However, in this set of scriptures, since righteousness has been satisfied, all of the Godhead is present and in full glory in this throne.

This is pictured in Genesis 1–3, showing all the Godhead being present during creation. Now, at the finish of time and the establishing of the eternal kingdom, all the Godhead is present. The Lamb has special mention here because He, as the Lamb, is the instrument of salvation. Please remember chapter 5. Hebrews 9:28 say, "So Christ was once offered to bear the sins of many." Wouldn't it have been nice if mankind could have gone from creation and the garden straight to this throne?

> *24. And the nations of them which are saved shall walk in the Light of it: and the kings of the earth do bring their glory and honour into it.*

169

25. And the gates of it shall not be shut at all by day:for there shall be no night there.

26. And they shall bring the glory and honour of the nations into it.

27. And there shall in no wise enter into it any thing that defileth, neither whatsoever worketh abomination, or maketh a lie: but they which are written in the Lamb's book of life.

Reservations only, please. That's right, and the One watching the book, we remember, is the Lamb Himself.

When we see the mentioning of kings and nations, I find myself wondering. The king's part, I don't mind, because chapter 5 mentions about making His believers kings and priests. We are called a royal priesthood already. Furthermore, we are children of God, which means we are kings already. The only people permitted in here are the saved and the ones who never made it to the age of accountability. We must understand that in God's eyes, there is not one person better than another.Take a moment and think of God's light shining off us and our crowns.

I think the nations' part of the verse is the fruit of our labor. So, where do these nations come from? The way I got it figured, it is the lineage of souls won. For instance, you won a soul, and that person won another person, and that person won another person, and so on. However, we all stand individually before God, yet we have the opportunity to win crowns and stars in those crowns. Oh, won't it be better to see folks in the New Jerusalem than at the white throne judgment?

Boy, that last verse is of great encouragement-no evil ever. It is a beautiful home. Are you ready for this home? The way I understand the Lamb's Book of Life is this: When God was ready to create mankind, He wrote everyone's name who would be conceived in His book. After we come to the age of accountability, we have an opportunity to accept Him. The problem is that some, most actually, refuse the salvation urgings of the Holy Spirit. Then at death, He blots those names out of the Lamb's Book of Life. Friend, we are nearing the end; you don't want your name blotted out. *Someone say amen!*

Chapter 22

1. And he shewed me a pure river of water of life, clear as crystal,, proceeding out of the throne of God and of the Lamb.

2. In the midst of the street of it, and on either side of the river, was there the tree of life, which bare twelve manner of fruits, and yielded her fruit every month: and the leaves of the tree were for the healing of the nations.

This takes us back to John, the fourth chapter. The Lord is talking to a woman about the living water that He could give her. Quite honestly, folks, why would our glorified bodies need water and the fruit and leaves of the Tree of Life? I think it has to do with fellowship. In amongst the grandeur of this scene, the providing God provides us with an opportunity for fellowship with Him and for community of the masses. Our glorified bodies will be eternal and have need of nothing, but eating is always a time of fellowship. This Baptist lov-v-ves dinners!

One other thought: If Adam had chosen the Tree of Life, could it have been possible to have skipped all this sin junk? Well, the Lord will answer these questions later, I reckon. Isn't it neat how the Lord uses the opportunity of food in the lives of the people of the Bible and in our lives? Food and sleep are the two main commodities of our lives. If we didn't have to eat, we would have a lot more money; if we didn't have to sleep, we would have a lot more time to spend that money. I like to do both.

Did you notice the yielding of the fruit every month? Even though there is no night there and time is not a factor anymore, the use of the reality of existence is still there. This may go back to Revelation 20:10. This next paragraph I meant to put in when I was discussing that particular verse. I'm glad I saved it for now, when discussing day and no night forever and ever.

When I became ill in the early part of 1998 from overexposure to hydrocarbons, I hurt so terribly. My sleeping times were mostly spent in my easy chair. I remember longing for the daylight to come; then, in the daylight, longing for the nighttime. The pain would just not go away. Now, in verse 10 of chapter 20, Lucifer and all his folks are going to be in the same boat, but with no relief ever. While in the New Jerusalem, we will be overjoyed as the months go by. Ain't God good?

> *3. And there shall be no more curse: but the throne of God and of the Lamb shall be in it; and his servants shall serve him:*
>
> *4. And they shall see his face; and his name shall be in their foreheads.*
>
> *5. And there shall be no night there; and they need no candle, neither Light of the sun; for the Lord God giveth them Light: and they shall reign for ever and ever.*

Just a thought here, considering that we reign forever and ever. Think about the use of the word kings in the earlier verses. In heaven, since we are children of God, it stands to reason that we are kings. A believer is a believer; and as such, we have been born again, and into the King's family. Boy, God just keeps stacking on the riches.

Do you remember the mention of mansions? Boy, what a scene God describes for us. We saw in verse 5 that we will reign forever and ever. There will be no work to do, just reigning. Now tell me why. Let's couple two things together: having fellowship with God and the fact that we have mansions. This tells me that our life there will be as if we are royalty. Guess what? We are royalty. We are children of the King. I really don't think we can fathom what heaven will be like. But God is trying to tell us:

1. There will be no more curse. Praise God, there will be no death, hunger, tiredness, hatred, deception, lust, anger, and any other negative thing we have in our lives today.

173

2. We will be in the presence of the true and living God, the only God there ever was. It says we will serve Him. I wonder what that will be like. I bet'cha I'll be able to sing there.

3. We will be able to gaze at and into the face of God. Now that's neat, and just think of it—we will belong. Most of our lives is spent trying to belong, to fit in with someone or something. No doubt about it, we will belong; we will have His name on our foreheads. You know, that makes it seem Well we are a piece of property. Well, we are just that; however, let's think of it a different way. It is so good to have someone who actually, totally cares for us. God does just that.

4. There will be no more night. Here on earth, night comes and we get our needed rest. Night comes and we need a light source. It kind of sow1ds like limitations, huh? Also, we don't know just what is in the darkness of our lives. It is nice to know that there will be no night, nor need of night there, nor need of an alternate light source.

5. The last clause of verse 5 says we will reign with God. You know, here on earth almost all humans go through life being reigned over and just trying to get by. We are not going to have reigning type duties, but we will have reigning type lives. The Bible says we are children of the King. Silly ol' Lucifer could havekept a veryspecial position. He's gonna' burn, and we are gonna' reign. Praise God!

6. *And he said unto me, These sayings are faithful and true: and the Lord God of the holyprophets sent his angel to shew unto his servants the things which must shortly be done.*

7. *Behold, I come quickly: blessed is he that keepeth the sayings of the prophecy of this book.*

God has just put His stamp of approval on what John has been shown. The Bible is from God and will be fulfilled. Fmthermore, the person who respects that and follows God is and will be happy.

> *8. And I John saw these things, and heard them. And when I had heard and seen, I fell down to worship before the feet of the angel which shewed me these things.*
>
> *9. Then saith he unto me, See thou do it not: for I am thy fellowservant, and of thy brethren the prophets, and of them which keep the sayings of this book: worship God.*

Tears fill my eyes to think of John falling to worship. The sights were so overwhelming that the only response he could muster was to fall in worship. John evidently had suffered so much for Christ. What a relief to see the beauty of the coming reward. Three times now John had been shaken to reality, and John was a seasoned veteran in hard or shocking times. The main thing to keep in mind is that no matter what, keep your eyes on the Lord. Trust His Word, and follow Him to the ends of the earth and to death. John had a lonely time on Patmos, and life has lonely times for all of us. But not *there!*

> *10. And he saith unto me, Sea not the sayings of the prophecy of this book: for the time is at hand.*
>
> *11. He that is unjust, let him be unjust still: and he which is filthy, let him be filthy still: and he that is righteous, let him be righteous still: and he that is holy, let him be holy still.*

The Book of Revelation is not a sealed book. We should educate our fellowman about its events. The time of the end of this era is near. Our time is short. Then we come to verse 11. We should not get bogged down in our efforts for one individual, even though each person is important. How many people could have been won if that same effort had been spent elsewhere? I used to try to be a "salesman," and verse 11 sure is true. *Besides, we are not the Holy Spirit.* Consider this: if the death part of life was a conveyor belt, how many people could we win? Limiting our time per person to five minutes would enable us to reach more people. Compare that to spending hours with the person who will *not* see.

I'm not saying that any one person is not worth all the time in the world. I'm saying that we should remember that a person will not and cannot get saved if God does not draw them. While God is holding salvation out to everyone, He knows when to draw them, and He knows if they are already past the drawing stage.

Verse 11 tells us that God's decisions will remain the same, no matter what we decide co do. If we in our brashness want to be unrighteous, it does not change God's mind. He will finish His creation purpose. Those who will deal with the "Man Upstairs" when they get there have already made an eternal decision. That, dear ones, is sad.

> *12. And, behold, I come quickly; and my reward is with me, to give every man according as his work shall be.*
> *13. I am Alpha and Omega, the beginning and the end, the first and the last.*

The Lordspeaks up and says, "Listen. I'm coming soon, and the rewards a person is due I'm bringing with Me. Be assured it is I, and I'm coming in all My grandem. Will you be ready and watching and working?"

> *14. Blessed are they that do his commandments, that they may have right to the tree of life, and may enter in through the gates into the city.*
> *15. For without are dogs, and sorcerers, and whoremongers, and murderers, and idolaters, and whosoever loveth and maketh a lie.*

John says happy is the person who accepts Christ as Savior, keeps His Word, and follows Him. The city will be great. Be assured, God will deal with sinners, as He has scheduled.

> *16. I Jesus have sent mine angel to testify unto you these things in the churches. I am the root and the offspring of David, and the bright and morning star.*

The Lord reiterates that it is He Himself who is telling of these things. He then gives His credentials: He is David's rightful heir to the throne, and Scripture calls Him the Light of all lights, "the *bright and morning star.*" In Revelation 3:7, He is *"the key."*

> 17. *And the Spirit and the bride say, Come. And let him that heareth say, Come. And let him that is a thirst come. And whosoever will let him take the water of life freely*

A totally intense invitation is given. The Holy Spirit and the bride urge the hearers to come to Christ. We are encouraged to extend the invitation to all of mankind. Then, looking back at verse 11, we see concerning those who are hungry for truth— I mean, real truth— *"let him that is athirst come."* Still looking at verse 11, we see, *"Whosoever will let him take the water o life freely"* We should be equally intense in our efforts to witness and win.

Time is so short. Are you looking for truth? Christ is extending salvation to you right now. He died to pay your sin debt in order to be able to offer you salvation by His grace. Have you prayed the sinner's prayer? Ask Christ to save you now.

> 18. *For I testify unto every man that heareth the words of the prophecy of this book, If any man shall add unto these things, God shall add unto him the plagues that are written in this book:*
> 19. *And if any man shall take away from the words of the book of this prophecy, God shall take away his part out of the book of life, and out of the holy city, and from the things which are written in this book.*

God knows all too well that evil will try to lessen the impact of His Word. God takes His Word and invitation most seriously. You may think you can get by with something, but remember the books of chapter 20 and the results.

20. He which testifieth these things saith, Surely I come quickly. Amen. Even so, come, Lord Jesus.
21. The grace of our Lord Jesus Christ be with you all. Amen.

The Lord uses the word *"surely."* He knows His schedule of times, and it has been two thousand years. His prophecies have been fulfilled. Time is short. Are we ready to encourage the Lord to come, as John did? *"Amen. Even so, come, Lord Jesus."*

Verse 21 expresses John's desire for us to be bathed in the grace of our Lord Jesus Christ. That is good for us as individuals. But we should also see that, that is where we are, and that we should have the same longing as John to share it. Thanks for listening, and I hope that some of your questions have been answered It's been fun.

"In hope of eternal life, which God, that cannot lie ..." (Titus 1:2)

Larry A. Heidelberg